LITERARY ESSAYS 1954–1974

Kennikat Press

National University Publications

Literary Criticism Series

General Editor
John E. Becker
Fairleigh Dickinson University

JAMES T. FARRELL

LITERARY ESSAYS

1954–1974

Collected and Edited by

JACK ALAN ROBBINS

National University Publications
KENNIKAT PRESS   //   1976
Port Washington, N. Y.   //   London

Manufactured in the United States of America

Published by
Kennikat Press Corp.
Port Washington, N.Y./London

"A Dreiser Revival" is reprinted from the book *Theodore Dreiser,* © 1962, 1963 by James T. Farrell. Used with permission of Dell Publishing Co., Inc. "Writer with Few Readers," "From Bunk to Buncombe," "Harvest of O'Faolain," "How Should We Rate Dos Passos?" and "A Veblen of the Novel" are reprinted by permission of *The New Republic,* © 1956, 1957, 1958, The New Republic, Inc. "William McFee" was published in the 1967 *Proceedings* of the American Academy of Arts and Letters, 17. "Sinclair Lewis" appeared in *The New Leader* of November 14, 1955. "The Writer—Neurotic or Psycotic?" "On Ignorance," and "Memories of New York" are printed with permission of *Park East.* "A Mencken Revival" is from *Prejudices: A Selection,* by H. L. Mencken, with an Introduction by James T. Farrell. Copyright © 1958 by Alfred A. Knopf, Inc. Reprinted by permission of the publisher. "George Ade: Creator of 'Artie' and 'Pink Marsh'" was first published by The University of Chicago Press. "A Paris Memoir" and "A Remembrance of Ernest Hemingway appeared in the *Chicago Daily News.* "The Eternal Question of John O'Hara" appeared in the *Toronto Telegram.*

Library of Congress Cataloging in Publication Data

Farrell, James Thomas, 1904–
James T. Farrell literary essays, 1954-1974.

(Literary criticism series)
(Kennikat Press national university publications)
1. American literature—History and criticism—Addresses, essays, lectures.
2. Literature—Addresses, essays, lectures.
I. Title.
PS121.F3   810'.9   76-17588
ISBN 0-8046-9125-8

CONTENTS

CONTENTS

III. REVIEWS

IV. ON THE CRAFT OF WRITING

EDITOR'S PREFACE

Editing a collection of James T. Farrell's writings is not an easy task. Farrell has been writing since 1926. Where does an editor begin and where should he leave off? Farrell has also been a very prolific writer on a wide range of topics—literature, politics, culture, history, language, and even baseball. In sheer weight, Farrell's occasional essays, journalism, and unpublished manuscripts are greater than his published twenty novels, eighteen short story collections, and five slender volumes of literary criticism.

In selecting the essays for inclusion in this book I have been guided by several thoughts. The last collection of Farrell's essays to appear in a hardcover edition was *Reflections at Fifty* in 1954. This left a gap of twenty years in which his rather devoted reading audience would have had to scan periodical indices to locate the occasional writings. Thus I felt it would be useful to bridge the 1954 to 1974 gap. Actually, this decision was not a very difficult one to make. Farrell is best known for his early novels: the *Studs Lonigan* trilogy (1932-1935), *A World I Never Made* (1936), *My Days of Anger* (1943) and *Bernard Carr* (1946). The collection of Farrell's short stories most widely read by college literature students of the past decade is an omnibus volume of his first three collections: *Calico Shoes* (1934), *Guillotine Party* (1935), and *Can All This Grandeur Perish?* (1937). The popularity of the early fiction is easily understandable but it does no justice to Farrell. The early fiction often embodies youthful, sometimes even adolescent, preoccupations and concerns. This is natural to novels and stories about young people growing into maturity, which does typify much of Farrell's early fiction. It also explains the perennial appeal of these novels and stories to youthful readers. (More than a few people I know have told me that *Studs Lonigan* helped them come to terms with their own transition to adulthood.)

This emphasis on the young Farrell, however, tends to overshadow the growth and maturity of the older writer, the author of *The Silence of History* (1963) and *A Brand New Life* (1968). Even more important, a focus on the early fiction may have had the effect of discouraging serious critics of literature from paying sufficient attention to the later novels and stories. To illustrate what I mean, I would recommend to the reader of this book that the stories in four particular short story collections be read for comparison: *Calico Shoes* (1934), *A Dangerous Woman* (1957), *Side Street* (1961), and *Judith* (1973). The reader will be able to see the improvement and maturity in the narrative style, concision of prose, characterization, and depth of understanding of concrete situations in the human condition. Speaking for myself, I readily admit to a preference for the later fiction because of the craftsmanship and artistic achievement.

It is almost embarrassing to read the early writings of either F. Scott Fitzgerald or William Faulkner, or James Jones. Ernest Hemingway was fortunate in having lost a trunkful of his early stories and poems. The short fiction of Bernard Malamud, a late starter, is distinguished by the clear maturity of concept and execution. The later writings of James T. Farrell evidence a similar maturity, essays as well as fiction.

For this book I have selected from among a great many of Farrell's literary essays, book reviews, reminiscences and other occasional writings since 1954. This is not intended to be a comprehensive collection but, rather, representative of Farrell at his best. These essays were chosen, then, largely with the consideration that in subject matter they are of enduring interest to readers of Farrell. I have been especially desirous of presenting Farrell's views on writers who have influenced him to a greater or lesser degree: Zola, Dreiser, Sinclair Lewis, H. L. Mencken, George Ade and Edgar Lee Masters. Farrell's comments on some of his contemporaries are quite provocative: Fitzgerald, Hemingway, John Dos Passos, Nelson Algren, John O'Hara and Archibald MacLeish. The essays on Oscar Wilde, Ben Hecht, Isaac Babel, Sean O'Faolain are illuminating. In the final section, "On the Craft of Writing," I have included a series of brief essays Farrell wrote on the vocation of the writer.

Throughout a span of nearly fifty years of serious writing James T. Farrell has remained faithful to his own conception of literature as art and of art as life. From *Young Lonigan* (1932) to *Invisible Swords* (1971), from his stories to his short poems, from the prose poem *When Time Was Born* to the experimental novel *New Year's Eve—1929*, this conception has been manifest. The essays in this collection as well, I believe, bear witness.

Jack Alan Robbins

May 1976

LITERARY ESSAYS 1954–1974

I
CRITICISM

A Mencken Revival

Introduction to *Prejudices*

I

During the last year or so, there have been signs of a Mencken revival. His books are selling well, and his name once again appears frequently in the press. I keep meeting intelligent younger people interested in his work and personality. The Mencken legend is being restored.

The time seems ripe for a Mencken revival. There are at least superficial resemblances between the present decade and the 1920s, when Mencken reached the peak of his influence. We are never without buncombe in the world, and today we have more than our share of it. Mencken was more than expert and witty in letting the air out of the buncombe artists. And, further, plutocracy is back both in the saddle and in the forefront of the national consciousness. With the aid of many hired publicity hands, plutocracy is seeking to restore some of the prestige and self-acknowledged honor which it enjoyed in the 1920s. And, while Mencken was conservative in his economic views, he only laughed at many of the pretensions of businessmen who turned money-making into a farcical pseudo religion of service, and sometimes into a ludicrous cult of Inspiration. Mencken would never have advocated that the wealth of the late Judge Elbert H. Gary be expropriated. All he did was to describe the big industrialist as though he were a nonentity. His respect for the Rockefellers was no greater. In Mencken's eyes, Gary, the Rockefellers, and Sam Gompers were all inferior men. Of the politician, Mencken had little good to say. With very, very few exceptions, he considered politicians a low order whom the citizen, at best, must bear in fortitude. Until 1936 he usually voted the Democratic ticket, except in 1924, when he cast his ballot for Senator Robert M. La Follette, Sr. He did not agree with La Follette's program or ideas, but he regarded the Wisconsin Senator as a rare bird in politics, an honest man who bravely refused to water down his convictions. Toward Harding, Coolidge, and "Lord Hoover" he was merciless. However, as late as 1934 he regarded President Franklin D. Roosevelt as a gentleman, "honest, gallant and mellowed." Soon after this his view of "Dr. Roosevelt" changed and he wrote of the man with bitterness, rather than with the contempt which he had for some of Roosevelt's predecessors. "Roosevelt Minor" became for him "a milch cow with 125,000,000 teats." Once when I was visiting Mencken during his long years of affliction, he spoke quite differently of President Eisenhower. He remarked: "That fellow has dignity. He's all right." As is known, some of Mencken's most demolishing work dealt with politicians.

Washington is as rich a field for a man of Mencken's talents today as it was in the 1920s. However, it is doubtful that a younger Mencken could now write with the directness and the fearless bluntness of H.L.M. and be published regularly. The conformity and the complacency which he scorned are more noticeable in our publications than at any other period in my own lifetime. There is now perhaps more relevance in Mencken's writing than during the 1930s or the war period. However, his work was always tonic and stimulating. We only reduce its buoyant force and the value and pleasure we can gain from it, if we think of Mencken as relevant merely to one or another selected era. Many of his essays, journalistic reports, sundry and miscellaneous writings have risen above and beyond their own time. Is his marvelous satire "Star-Spangled Men" pertinent only to the 1920s? If we interpret Mencken merely as a man of the gaudy, crazy twenties, we will see him only in part. Mencken has always been a stimulating and valuable writer.

II

Mencken shocked an delighted a generation of college students who read *The American Mercury*. But there were and there are values for the mature in Mencken's work. In the twenties he did not write solely for sophomores. He reflected and became a voice for values superior to those which had had such wide currency, not only among the species "boobus Americanus" but also on college campuses and in editorial offices and the realm of the so-called mighty. This might be obscured because of Mencken's ex-cathedra manner, because of his over-generalizations, his humor,

[6]

and his frequent reliance on the argument of *reductio ad absurdum,* which he often handled not only cleverly but even brilliantly. Furthermore, a realization of Mencken's role in fighting for major values can easily be lost by those who react quickly to his anti-democratic views.

Mencken continually declared that he wrote for "the civilized minority." He meant those who believed in and were interested in ideas and the play of the mind. He meant those whose taste for literature was for books in which you could find truth, a sense of reality, a feeling for the complexities and inexplicableness of men and of their varied destinies. He held the eighteenth century in high esteem, and undoubtedly associated himself with it. In 1931, when writing in *The American Mercury* on "The New Architecture," he stated: "The Eighteenth Century . . . had its defects, but they were vastly overshadowed by its merits. It got rid of religion. . . . It introduced urbanity into manners, and made even war relatively gracious and decent. It took eating and drinking out of the stable and put them into the parlor. It found the sciences childish curiosities, and bent them to the service of men, and elevated them above metaphysics for all time."

His idea of "the civilized minority," of an intellectual aristocracy, was as definitely influenced by the eighteenth century as it was by the Nietzschean idea of the superman. The ideal of reason or rationality and of impersonal causation is at the core of Mencken's thought and his writing. He was a far-off derivative of the Enlightenment, and in twentieth-century America he played something of the role of a Voltaire. In addition, he was a convinced Darwinian. And, despite the rather freewheeling manner in which he made blanket, all-inclusive statements, Mencken could and did think well. Those who declare that he was a great humorist, but minimize his capacities of ratiocination are, I believe, not quite accurate about him. Many of these *Prejudices* show us a man with a strong mind as well as a vigorous, virile spirit full of gusto. His ideas and views became fixed early in life, and, admittedly, he held to his biases and prejudices. He changed his opinions, but never his basic views. Thus, one of his gorgeous essays is "The Sahara of the Bozart," which is included in this selection. He later somewhat revised his views of the South and saw some changes in that region. After having characterized Hollywood as "Moronia," he met a number of intelligent people in the motion-picture industry and accordingly revised his opinion of it.

These essays reveal that Mencken had a ranging, curious mind. Also, while his basic views on democracy, on economics, liberty, and reason were firm and practically immovable, he was a reasonable man, ready to recognize grounds for changing his mind on many matters of interpretation. People who knew him and corresponded with him encountered many instances of this.

Mencken's views, so challengingly and excitingly expressed in these essays, were well formed in the early 1900s. From then on, he largely saw in American life evidence to confirm his own ideas. The attitudes from a Victorian-Puritan past were still powerful in America during the early years of this century. Many sentimentalities, pieties, childish and banal simplicities of McGuffey's Readers remained gospel for millions. A colonialized Victorianism with its moral piety was still exerting a suffocating influence in the literary world. Liberation of the mind from the vestiges of this colonialism and the taboos of an over-conventionalized moralism was far from complete. We frequently read of the American tradition as a liberal one of fair play and tolerance. This is but a partial truth. From the frontier and through Lincoln, Mark Twain, and Walt Whitman, as well as from the Founding Fathers, we do derive a tradition that is liberal. It should be added here that Mencken rejected the ideas of the historian Frederick Jackson Turner. He saw anew that there was much illiberalism, intolerance, and bigotry in the American past. Especially in small towns and the countryside, narrow-mindedness was rampant. America is so vast that almost everything said about it is likely to be true, and the opposite is probably equally true. Mencken in these *Prejudices* recognized and described much that is true about American life.

From the final years of the nineteenth century onward, America received new and fresh whiffs from Europe. In the arts, one of the agents of this influence was James Huneker, a friend and to some degree an inspirer of Mencken. Also, this was a period when the city triumphed over the country. The superiority of the values of the city over those of the rural areas is crucial and central in these essays, as well as in much of Mencken's other writing. He saw issues of freedom of speech, scientific truth versus superstition, and even the phenomenon of Prohibition as part of the conflict between city and country. This explains one of the wittiest essays of this collection, "The Husbandman." And a recent volume of Mencken's journalistic articles on politics. *A Carnival of Buncombe,* reiterates this point. Thus, he wrote in 1928:

"But the battle for Prohibition was more than a struggle for a moral reform: it was also a clear-cut combat between cities and the country, between the civilized centers and the areas of cornbread and revival."

Above all else, you will find here Mencken as a liberating voice.

These essays originally strenghened the will of a generation to think independently, to write with greater truth and conviction. He challenged those forces in American life which would have repressed honesty. He dramatically satirized the preposterous, including the malignantly preposterous. He handled and manhandled manners and pieties which stood as barriers to a free development. In addition, his writing is just plain good fun and excitement.

III

"Carlyle was right. The only solution is work." This was a remark which Mencken often made to his friends. With all his vigor and ribaldry, Mencken was, in fact, a strongly pessimistic man. Something of that deep pessimism which intelligent men drew as a conclusion from Darwinism and nineteenth-century determinism was fixed in his nature. He was a rebel in spirit, but not a reformer. He did not believe that either man or society could be much improved. He regarded this life as all that man can ever know, and he had no illusions about it. In his long and rather famous essay "On the National Letters," published in 1919, Mencken criticized popular American fiction of the time on the ground that its usual hero was a second-rate man who struggled to achieve inferior and unsatisfactory ends of material success. In contrast to "the typical American hero" of the success novel, he wrote of the hero of first-class or great fiction as a "man of reflective habits." And "what interests this man is the . . . poignant and significant conflict between a salient individual and the harsh and meaningless forces of destiny, the indestructible mandates and vagaries of God." Here Mencken was actually referring to more than the hero of significant fiction: he was writing of his own inner feeling about life. This, I believe, is the reason why he was so frequently prompted to remark that work was the only solution. At the same time, he was a man who loved his work. He loved writing and reading. He liked writers, too, even though he poked fun at them. He saw them as part of "the civilized minority," and infinitely superior to politicians. He also genuinely enjoyed helping them. In his "Notebooks," published posthumously as *Minority Report,* he jotted down the following:

"I know a great many more people than most men, and in wider and more diverse circles, yet my life is essentially one of isolation, and so is that of every other man. We not only have to die alone; we also, save for a few close associates, have to live alone. I have been able, in my time, to give help to a good many young authors, male and female, and some of them have turned out very well. I often think of the immense number of others that I might have aided if I had only known of them."

I was the last, or at least one of the last, younger writers whom Mencken published in *The American Mercury*. In April 1932, five days before my first novel, *Young Lonigan,* was published, my wife and I arrived in New York from Paris. We had about ten dollars, which we spent on that first day. But the next morning I learned that Mencken had bought a story of mine, "Helen I Love You." I received one hundred dollars for it, and it was published in *The American Mercury*. From then on I corresponded with Mencken until he was stricken in 1948. His letters always came promptly in answer to mine. Many of them were brief, but he was usually to the point. These letters covered a range of subjects—literature, political oratory and style, Napoleon, language and slang. I first met Mencken one night in August 1935. I was passing the Hotel Brevoort with Hortense Alden, and she remarked that there was Mencken. He was sitting at a table with Edgar Lee Masters. I introduced myself, and he invited us to sit down. We drank beer and talked for about an hour. Mencken and Masters were good friends, and they enjoyed each other's company. They liked to joke about Bryan, the Fundamentalists, and the yokels, and they did so that evening. Perhaps because I was a younger man, Mencken spoke of his own earlier days. He mentioned Richard Harding Davis as a great reporter of that era, and talked of the Kipling of *Barrack Room Ballads*. And he predicted that Huey Long would be assasssinated. It was a most pleasant evening.

I next saw Mencken at the Republican National Convention in Cleveland in 1936. As conventions go, it was a very dull one. But it was my first, and I lapped it up, undoubtedly because I had been influenced by Mencken's descriptions. No one but the Kansans took Governor Landon seriously. But they, endlessly singing "Oh Susannah," believed as firmly that Landon would be the next President of the United States as William Jennings Bryan believed in the tenets of Fundamentalism.

At a convention Mencken was not as flamboyant as he is sometimes said to have been. He worked seriously and stayed longer at his seat in the press section than many of the other working reporters. If he had to get his story off when a session closed, he would not stop to drink, but would go to his typewriter. When I watched him, he didn't take many notes. At Cleveland, and again at the 1936 Democratic Convention in Philadelphia, I happened to sit next to him at a number of the sesssions. Usually wearing

[10]

a seersucker suit, he would look out at the swarm of delegates with his glasses sliding down on his nose, his eyes twinkling, and his face lighted up with amusement and interest. In Philadelphia in 1936 I sat next to him on the hot, dull day when President Roosevelt was renominated. The platform was crowded with politicians from every corner of the land. One after another, they got in on the act with seconding speeches. This went on for hours and hours and was carried into the night. The floor emptied of delegates, who went off to the ball game, to the saloons, to any place less depressing and boring than the Convention Hall. For on that day the record for an all-time low in the history of political oratory was undoubtedly established. Not one cliché was missed. The platitudes were deadly. The English language was raped. One after another, the politicians came to the rostrum and contributed their bits to the obscene ritual. Included among them was Happy Chandler; no one outdid him. This was a Mencken day, a Mencken scene on the convention floor. Like the delegates, the newspapermen had flown the coop. They were paid to work, but this was too much for them. But I sat it out with Mencken, fascinated. Perhaps the writings of Mencken back in the twenties impelled me. We listened in glee and amazement. He kept shaking his head, peering at the crowd of politicians on the platform. Finally he nudged me.

"Farrell, do you see all of those politicians up there?"

He pointed.

"Every one of them thinks that he can be President of the United States."

In 1945 my brother and I went from Washington to Baltimore to have lunch with Mencken. As he took us to his club, he half apologized, explaining that he had lambasted it and the other members but that he had found it more convenient to meet people for lunch there than at home. He was, needless to say, most gracious in his concern about what we ate and how we liked the food. He was a genuine gentleman.

Mencken was a good and fluent talker, and he had much to say that day. Because my brother was a doctor, Mencken spoke of medicine and insanity. He asserted his belief that eventually science would prove that insanity was caused by a condition in the blood; he expatiated on this theory. He also spoke of Ezra Pound, then but recently committed to St. Elizabeth's Hospital.

Mencken had visited Pound, taking along an armful of books of poetry. He'd told the doctor that the books were all poetry, "as bad as Ezra's." Mencken did not admire most poetry, as is well known. However, he was one of the first writers to visit Pound. This was characteristic of him. He would often do such things. He never knew Leon Trotsky and had no great respect for the man. However, when Trotsky was in exile in Prinkipo, Mencken read that there had been a fire in his home and that Trotsky's library was said to have been destroyed. Mencken wrote to Trotsky, offering to send him some books. Later, in Mexico, I discussed American writers with Trotsky, and he mentioned Mencken and that letter. Asking about Mencken, Trotsky said that he had never answered the letter. Why should he have accepted books from Mencken? The letter to Trotsky came into our conversation at Baltimore. Mencken made little of it. Trotsky's not having replied did not trouble him. He said that, having read of the fire, he had offered to send Trotsky some books that he might need for his work. But Trotsky, so often a gracious and impeccably polite man in personal relationships, was too haughty to respond to what was a friendly and impersonal gesture.

At that time, blood and blood pressure were on Mencken's mind. For, after having spoken of blood as the possible source or cause of insanity, he mentioned President Roosevelt, who had died two months previously.

"Jesus, his blood pressure must have been way up," Mencken said.

A few moments later he again mentioned Roosevelt's blood pressure. And then, after about five minutes more, he said:

"In four years I'll have a stroke and die."

I laughed at him and said that I didn't believe it. He insisted that this would happen. His stroke came about six months short of four years later, and it almost killed him.

He also spoke of books and writers, and remarked that, in the end, perhaps only scenes remained as great literature. This was the case, he said, with *Babbit* and also with what he considered to be Dreiser's best work. Mencken had affection for Dreiser, but regarded the man as a peasant. He remarked that if Dreiser became ill, and walked along a street where there were two signs, one reading Dr. Osler and the other Dr. Quack, you could bet all your money that Dreiser would go in to Dr. Quack every time.

It was when we were walking back to the railroad station that he suddenly asked:

"Farrell, how old are you?"

I told him forty-one. He said that I was young, had a wonderful future, and would possibly still write my best books.

"Farrell, if you want to develop further as a writer, there are three

[12]

things to stay away from. Booze . . . women . . . and politics."

These, he insisted, killed a literary talent. He mentioned Ring Lardner, whom he had seen often. Lardner, he said, would sit for hours, drinking in a morose silence.

Luncheon with Mencken was always a happy event.

IV

It was a gray fall afternoon in the period after Mencken had had a cerebral hemorrhage. I stopped off in Baltimore and took a cab to his house in Hollins Street. Mencken, wearing a blue suit, met me at the door. He did not look ill. In fact, he appeared hale and healthy. But then I realized definitely that he had become an old man. The first question he asked was:

"How are my friends?"

We went to his office or workroom and talked.

"I'm out of it. I'm finished. I wish I were dead."

He explained that he could no longer work. He was unable to read or write. The only thing he could do was help his secretary, who was arranging his correspondence, which was to go to a library.

Mencken's stroke, suffered in the fall of 1948, destroyed or affected the association tracts in his brain. He had great difficulty in remembering proper nouns or names. While I was with him on this occasion and later, he said that he knew me and remembered my books. But he didn't know my name; after I told it to him, he said he remembered.

"If I could read and write, I'd be content," he said. "I'm out of it."

He described how he lived. In spring he did some work in his garden. He and his brother August collected boxes and pieces of wood in the alley, and he broke them up. He went to some movies. During the first years he could go to Florida or be driven around Baltimore. Later he could not go out much. He would look out at the park or square in front of his home, watch the people in it, watch the children coming home from school, guess and speculate about them and their ages. He would walk around and talk to the Negro children in the neighborhood. Every afternoon he took a nap, and he went to bed early.

"I listen to the machine, the machine upstairs," he said, pointing upward. "The machine, they're all morons."

He meant the radio.

And people. He spoke of "the publisher." He meant Alfred Knopf, who would visit him. And "his friend," the "drama critic." It was George Jean Nathan. So it went. As soon as the name was supplied him, his memory functioned. He also mentioned books he'd like to reread. And there was the refrain in his conversation: he was out of it. And the second refrain: he would just as soon be dead. But, considering what had happened to him, his condition was good.

His voice was just a bit thick. Sometimes the wrong word would come. After a period of conversation his thoughts would wander. He was aware of this, and even commented on it. For two or three minutes we would speak of another subject. Then he would pick up the threads of the conversation.

He spoke, also, of the night when he had his stroke while at a restaurant in Baltimore. His description conveyed a sense of sick agony. But he was realistic and resigned about his condition. He had, in a sense, suggested his own final days, years before, when he had written of the hero of major fiction, a superior man, "a salient individual" in conflict with "harsh and meaningless fiats of destiny." His biological tragedy, this harshness of his destiny, was all the more cruel and punishing because he was deprived of his main surcease—his work.

On that first visit after his stroke, we talked for a long time, perhaps two hours. It was dark out when I left. He accompanied me to the door and reminded me to tell his friends that he was doing well. But after a pause he added:

"Remember me to my friends. Tell them I'm a hell of a mess."

Such were the last days of H.L. Mencken. He bore them with courage.

V

It should be clear to the reader that the preparation of this volume was to me a joy, a labor of love, and a privilege. These selections are all taken from Mencken's six volumes of *Prejudices,* which were published between 1919 and 1927. A number of them, however, appeared first in *The Smart Set* or *The American Mercury.* They represent Mencken when he was at the peak of his influence and had, in fact, become a legend. Here is some of his wittiest and most buoyant writing. Something of his wide range of interests and his broad field of reference is to be found in these essays. Many of them are unforgettable. Here, in my opinion, is some of the very best of H.L. Mencken.

I was not guided by any one principle of selection. I chose what I liked and what I think and hope will be enjoyable to old and new readers of Mencken. It had been my desire to avoid any duplication of the selection in Alistair Cooke's excellently edited *The Vintage Mencken.* However, there are a few duplications of pieces just too good and impressive to omit. The Cooke volume, let me add, unlike this one, draws from the entire body of Mencken's writings. Also, I should like to call special attention to the essays on George Jean Nathan and James Huneker. These men were his friends. His name is bound up with theirs.

Here, then, is a selection from Mencken's *Prejudices.* I hope these writings may give others as much pleasure as they have given me over the years stretching back to my own youth.

1958

On Oscar Wilde's *De Profundis*

Somewhere in Proust's account of Swann in love there is the phrase "this inhuman world of pleasure." And recently when I happened to pick up Oscar Wilde's *De Profundis,* this phrase came to me. It seemed so applicable to the pathetic story of Oscar Wilde. Other than his "Ballad of Reading Gaol" and his poem "The Harlot's House," which moved me in my youth, I never had much taste for his writing; his wit seems somewhat artificial. His *fin siècle* appears shallow and too closely bound up with the Victorian world which he flaunted. But at that, the so-called yellow decade has influenced us all more than we have always realized. It stands behind our formative years, the 1920s; and in that period, it was considered more important than it is today. Just as Wilde seems limited, shallow if clever, and affected, so does Aubrey Beardsley, with his drawings of a figure of woman compouned of a suggestion of evil and strangeness. But this decade marked the end of an era as well as of a century.

The revolt against Victorianism was not unmerited or unwarranted. The laughter, the contempt, the anger which Victorianism has stirred through the decades of this century have been too continuing and too persistent to be treated as unmerited. It was an age of evasions and hypocrisies. Human nature was not seen with clear and frank eyes. False hopes were generated in men and a perhaps undue optimism developed. The breakup of the Victorian world and the refutation of its optimistic hopes produced a brittleness and a pessimism that have run deep in the minds and feelings of more than one generation. The Victorian world, however, was not as happy a world as it might seem in retrospect. Sadness and doubt struggled with hope; this can be seen in the writing of the time. One of the big shocks of the Victorian era was that of Darwinism, and its shock was registered on the intellectual convictions and certainties of men. There is a questioning of purpose, a melancholy, and a doubt in some of the writing of the time. The poetry of Matthew Arnold is melancholy and this mood is eloquently registered in his beautiful poem "Dover Beach." In Tennyson, the purpose of life is often questioned. The optimism of Browning sometimes has a hollow note.

But there was a vigor and a breadth of interest in the great Victorians and as the century drew to its end, this vigor declined.

The new spirit was one of revolt but of a revolt with less vigor and virility than the earlier writers showed. In Oscar Wilde, there is cleverness and sometimes brilliance, but no vigor. A conception of art took the place of a conception of life and art became the purpose of life. Art and revolt were more or less synonymous. But this spirit of revolt was a little too elegant to be real and deep-seated. To shock the Philistines was more important than to understand and to reveal. To be brilliant was more important than to be sound. The *bon mot* was another yellow flower to be flaunted. The dandy posed as a kind of revolutionary, but he remained a dandy tied to the world he shocked and flaunted.

The philistinism which Wilde abhorred was more deeply rooted, more mean-spirited, and more vindictive than he realized. His surprise and the description of his sorrow in *De Profundis* suggest this. The cruel and wholly unwarranted treatment of Wilde more than exposes the viciousness and malignancy of this philistinism.

Wilde was made a martyr because of his private life. Vindictiveness wore a mean mask of justice. A child more than a man, this was enough to break him. After his release from prison, he lived out his days pitifully and pathetically. The image of Wilde grown fat, aging, and sitting over an absinthe in a Paris café is wrought with pathos. Only a few short years before, he had been the toast of London. An aura of brilliance had surrounded him. He had been the golden boy riding a golden wave.

There are many sayings, many commonplaces and banalities about fame and its hollowness. I do not wish to add to them, but still, I cannot resist wondering if fame was ever more hollow than it was in the case of Oscar Wilde.

We who live at a later date in a freer age can only look back on this episode with a feeling of frustrated disgust. "The wrong of unshapely things," wrote Yeats, "is a wrong too great to behold." This was an unshapely wrong, all the more unshapely because Wilde was Irish; his mother was a friend of Irish patriots and in the English upper classes, the Irish were seen as a low and troublesome care. The persecution of Oscar Wilde followed on the publication of the Pigott forgeries. It happened in the same decade as did the Parnell debacle.

When it was too late and Oscar Wilde had gone pitifully to his grave, a broken man, sympathies changed. Today, he is remembered as a symbol; his persecution and imprisonment have, if anything, helped his reputation as a writer. But in that day, virtue was never more than in its triumph over Oscar Wilde.

"Suffering," Wilde wrote in the beginning of *De Profundis,* "is one long moment." So it must have seemed to him while he was in Reading Gaol. In another part of this book, he speaks of the monotony of prison life. A sense of this same monotony was movingly expressed in "The Ballad of Reading Gaol."

The long moment of Wilde's suffering was new to him. As we know, and as he stated in *De Profundis,* he had lived for pleasure. He quotes two lines of Wordsworth which he believed he had come to understand better than Wordsworth himself had:

Suffering is permanent, obscure, dark
And has the nature of infinity.

All through *De Profundis* there are sentences about suffering:

"Pain, unlike pleasure, wears no mask."

"There are times when sorrow seems to me to be the only truth." In sorrow, he came to see "an extraordinary reality." Suffering was the secret "hidden behind everything."

Confessing that he had determined to know nothing of pain and sorrow, he then came to believe that he was forced to taste each of the bitter sorrows of life; and for a season, to have no other food but these. In all of this, Wilde seems to have been trying to come to terms with himself, and to have assimilated his experiences and to have handled the shock of his disgrace and humiliation.

Alternately, he expounded his feelings with a generalized metaphor about sorrow and pain and went down on his knees, as it were, to feel contrition.

There is an emotional poverty in *De Profundis.* Wilde's thoughts and observations are all strung on the theme of suffering. His spirit shrinks with his own suffering. There are more metaphors about suffering than there are insights into what suffering is and what it does to a person. The metaphors are a screen for a poverty of feeling.

"My only mistake was that I confined myself so exclusively to the trees of what seemed to be the sun-lit side of the garden, and shunned the other side for its shadow and gloom."

The question of style is here related (as is usually the case) to the man and his character. The metaphors of Wilde are often romantic and traditional.

He concludes his book by observing that while society will have no place for him, nature will. " . . . Nature, whose sweet rains fall on unjust and just alike, will have clefts in the rocks where I may hide, and secret valleys in whose silence I may weep undisturbed. She will hand the night with stars so that I may walk abroad in the darkness without stumbling, and send the wind over my footprints so that none can track me to my hurt; she will cleanse me in great waters, and with bitter herbs make me whole."

And "where there is sorrow, there is holy ground. Some day people will realize what that means. They will know nothing of life until they do."

And in his sorrow, an act of understanding and sympathy by a friend "made the desert blossom like a rose" and brought him "out of the bitterness of lonely exile into harmony with the wounded, broken, and great hearts of the world."

The feeling revealed in such passages is conventional, even sentimental. It is self-pity expressed melliferously without any individualizing insights. What Oscar Wilde lost in prison was not character but his feelings. And these were under-developed. The sentimentality and the conventional character of some of the metaphors, the characterizations of sorrows, cast a backward glance on his wit. It was not only a wit to shock and scandalize; it was a wit of evasion; an evasion of self and an escape from the hard and painful task of gaining insight. At one time, Wilde remarked that the purpose of art was to conceal art. His art was bound up with a concealing of insight, a mask for a poverty of insight.

But the emotional poverty and the conventionality of *De Profundis* is but part of the book. There is more; there is both real pain and suffering and affectation, side by side. Wilde remarked that "the supreme vice" was shallowness. At times, he himself was shallow. And at other times, a spirit in agony, a man with feeling and artistic ability spoke out of real suffering:

When I was in Wandsworth prison, I longed to die. It was my own desire. When after two months in the infirmary I was transferred here and found myself growing gradually better in physical health, I was filled with rage. I determined to commit suicide on the very day on which I left prison. After a time that evil mood passed away and I made up my mind to live, but to wear gloom as a king wears purple: never to smile again: to turn whatever house I entered into a house of mourning: to make my friends walk slowly in sadness with me: to teach them that melancholy is the true secret of life: to mar them with my own pain. Now I feel quite differently. I see it would be both ungrateful and unkind of me to pull so long a face that when my friends come to see me they would have to make their faces still longer in order to show their sympathy: or if I desired to entertain them, to invite them to sit down quietly to bitter herbs and baked meats. I must learn how to be cheerful and happy.

De Profundis shows Wilde struggling to be cheerful and to gain insight and a sense of integration in the face of a shattering experience. It also reveals him sinking into a self-pity which weakened a nature without sufficient inner fortitude. A man of pleasure who could not control his passions, self-pity was perhaps inevitable when he was so cruelly imprisoned. A gifted child, the darling of the drawing room, he was ill-equipped to withstand the humiliation of imprisonment. There are flashes of insight and feeling scattered through the book, but the recurrent note of self-pity is more evident.

An interesting part of *De Profundis* is where Wilde wrote of Christ, whom he regarded as belonging with the romantic poets: "I see a far more intimate connection between the true life of Christ and the true life of the artist."

He discerned in Christ "that close union of personality with perfection" that formed "the real distinction between the classical and romantic movements in life."

Christ, according to Wilde, possessed a nature precisely like that of the artist. His was an "intense and flamelike imagination." "Imaginative sympathy . . . the sole secret of creation," was realized by Christ in the entire sphere of human relations. Christ belonged with the poets. It was incredible to think that this young Galilean should imagine that he could bear on his shoulders the burden of the entire world. Coming in contact with his personality, the ugliness of people's sins were shed, and they came to realize the beauty of their sorrows. Nothing in Greek tragedy touches that of Christ or reveals such "pity and terror." Christ is a tragic figure who possessed absolute purity, and this fact raised his story to a height of

[20]

romantic art beyond the art of the Greeks. His whole life is an idyll. Christ's own renaissance "produced the Cathedral at Chartres, the Arthurian Cycle legends, the life of St. Francis of Assissi, the art of Goethe, and Dante's *Divine Comedy.* But it was not allowed to develop and was spoiled by the dreary classical Renaissance that gave us Petrarch, the Raphaels, Frescoes, and Palladian architecture, and formal French tragedy, and St. Paul's cathedral, and Pope's poetry."

The observations on Christ and the cathedral judgments reveal the willfulness of taste in Wilde. His claims concerning Christ are extravagant and irrelevant. Christ is appropriated to the tendency in art which Wilde saw as his own. However, his observations on the tragedy of Christ and on Christ's imagination remain interesting and suggestive. They help us see what is often overlooked—the quality and depth of humanity in Christ's sympathy. By characterizing Christ's life and suffering as a tragic and romantic work of art, Wilde brings into focus experiences and sayings of Christ and the tragic story of the crucifixion.

Wilde is identifying himself with Christ. He is, as it were, forging a link between his suffering and Christ's larger and widely symbolic passion and death. This is done indirectly and in the name of art. Wilde saw himself as an artist in life, and to see Christ through this framework of art was only in consonance with the way he saw life in general.

But try as he did, Wilde could not see his own suffering in these terms. *De Profundis* contains resolutions and expressions of determination to accept himself and to find a new integration. In this, he does not succeed. And his last lonely days were pathetic. His stay in Reading Gaol broke him.

Wilde was like a willful child. *De Profundis* suggests this in its emotional level. The reactions, the weeping are child-like. There are natures too frail for this world, natures which cannot withstand adversity, and they break in the face of it. Such was Oscar Wilde's nature. *De Profundis* records the last efforts of that nature to hold together before it broke and fell apart. The injustice and cruelty which led to the imprisoning of and the breaking of Oscar Wilde was Society's doing. But the way he faced this injustice was as much an expression of Oscar Wilde as were his comedies.

I say this descriptively, not in condemnation. It is not for me or any of us to condemn Oscar Wilde. Suffering made him a figure to arouse our feelings of compassion. But suffering did not send him forth a deeper and more mature artist. Rather, suffering brought into clear light the limitations in both the nature and the art of Oscar Wilde. It showed the immaturity of his revolt and the evasive character of his wit. A highly self-centered man, his art and his nature were sadly impregnated with too much of that which he saw as a supreme vice—shallowness. *De Profundis* was an effort to escape from shallowness. But only in a few parts is there any escape.

This but adds to the pathos in the story of Oscar Wilde.

1959

Ernest Hemingway

I

Between any critic and Hemingway's work is the Hemingway myth. But to allow this myth to distort the facts demeans literature and is a disservice to Hemingway, the writer.

Ernest Hemingway was born in Oak Park, Illinois, a suburb of Chicago, in 1898. Upon his graduation from Oak Park High School, he went to Kansas City, Missouri, and got a job as a cub reporter on the *Kansas City Star.*

Hemingway did not stay in this job long but his experience here was valuable in developing his consciousness as a writer. The rules for writing on the *Star* emphasized simplicity of style. This stuck with Hemingway. In 1918, he went to Italy as an ambulance driver. This seems to have been the only way he could get into the First World War.

He saw suffering and death. He saw men in pain, agony. They were wounded, maimed. Some were blown to bits. War was not romantic; it was violence at its most intense stage. The War and the wounds which he himself received had a traumatic effect on Ernest Hemingway, one to which he admitted. It influenced his entire literary career, especially his beginning years. Hemingway suffered multiple wounds from fragments of an exploding mortar. His kneecap was all but detached from his leg. He spent months convalescing. He had a love affair with a nurse in the hospital, an experience he wrote about in *A Farewell to Arms.* Originally, the story was "A Very Short Story" and was included in *In Our Time.* In the story, the nurse does not die.

Ernest Hemingway seems to have returned from the war with divided feelings. He was invited to speak at the Oak Park High School about his war experience. During his speech, he held up his army breeches with the holes from the mortar fragments that had caused his wounds. He spoke as though the war had been an exciting adventure. But in his story "Soldier's Home" he describes a returning soldier and his bitter attitude.

"Krebs went to war from a Methodist College in Kansas."

And Krebs comes home too late to be received as a hero. War hysteria had ebbed. Soldiers had returned to a hero's welcome earlier. At first, Krebs would not talk about the war but then he changed. He talked and talked. But the actualities of the war did not interest the townspeople. So Krebs lied; he exaggerated and invented atrocity stories. But then a distaste for his war experiences starts to set in. He feels a "nausea in regard to experience that is the result of untruth or exaggeration." Krebs was disassociated from his past and he wanted neither complications nor consequences. But he could not avoid them. His mother talks to him about settling down. He answers her bluntly, telling her that he has no ambition and that he can no longer pray. She begins to cry. In order to soothe her, he tells her "white lies." He decides to go to Kansas City and get a job. This results in another blowup because he won't, as his mother has asked him to do, go to his father's office and talk things over. "He wanted his life to go smooth."

We know that Kreb's life won't go smooth. The violent truths of his war experiences have made it impossible for him to live in his hometown the way that he is expected to live.

It is not necessary to assume that Krebs is an image of Hemingway himself to recognize that this story reveals an underlying interpretation of Hemingway's experience.

II

Ernest Hemingway came upon the American literary scene with his style perfected. In it, there was both simplicity and simplification. Behind that style there was a sensibility that was often poetic. There are many instances in his earlier writings where there seems to be an aura of the unsaid as part of the atmosphere which his writing evokes. He used common idiomatic expressions as a literary language. His dialogue, although highly stylized, seemed fresh and spontaneous.

[24]

Ernest Hemingway exercises a pronounced influence on American writers, particularly younger ones. The generation that followed him (and I am one of these) is much in his debt. Although many of his early stories and novels were set in locales far away and foreign to America, he helped to turn eyes to the common familiar scenes about one. His use of idiom also had this effect.

Hemingway concerned himself with techniques. He was one of the few American writers who wrote about war with a technical understanding. This shows in *For Whom the Bell Tolls* which is, otherwise, a poor and inflated novel. The topographical descriptives in this book constitute some of its redeeming features.

Techniques in boxing, hunting, fishing, or in bull fighting—these were things about which Hemingway knew something. And he applied his knowledge to his fiction. Just as Sherwood Anderson looked upon writing as a craft, Hemingway was inclined to regard it as a technique and he dedicated effort to perfecting his style. But Hemingway did not give himself an opportunity to grow. And growth is required for a writer's lasting stature.

Hemingway's first book of short stories made it clear that there was a new writer in American letters. But his later work, *The Old Man and the Sea,* shows no growth and development. There is much good writing in it but Hemingway had already proven that he could write well with his first book. And, *The Old Man and the Sea* was conceptually contrived. The Old Man is almost devoid of social relationships. His life, with borrowed symbolism, is a partial symbolism.

Hemingway's best years were his first ones. This is a personal view that I have long held and it is one which I retain even now when he is no more. And yet, I was of the opinion that he might write his greatest book as one of his last works; it was my hope that he would. No artist likes to see another artist decline.

The Hemingway who will last is the early Hemingway. In addition to the value of the books themselves, we must remember that these works exerted influence on other writers.

Ernest Hemingway was not in vain.

1961

A Dreiser Revival

Introduction to the *Laurel Dreiser*

I

There are many signs that the major works of Theodore Dreiser are once again gaining in admiration, and that the place he should occupy in American and world literature of the twentieth century is beginning to receive a new recognition. A number of his books are now in print, not only in hard cover but also in paperback editions. Even though much has been written about Dreiser, and despite the fact that I have written many essays and given several lectures about his career and his work, it is decidely appropriate to introduce Dreiser anew, especially for those who have yet to discover his books—but also as a refresher to others, whose familiarity with his work has grown dull with the rust of the years upon their memories.

Nine years from now, the centennial anniversary of Theodore Dreiser's birth will occur. I am inclined to think that when that time comes, his memory and his books will have acquired a greater popularity and respect than he ever knew when he was alive. By a coincidence, it so happens that I began this *Introduction* on the ninetieth anniversary of Dreiser's birth. It was in the early hours of a Sunday morning, August 27, 1961. Ninety years ago, on this same date, he was born in Indiana. His was a huge family. His father, John Paul Dreiser, was an immigrant from the German Rhineland, a man of strict probity, a Catholic who, according to Theodore Dreiser, became far more interested in the salvation of the souls of his children in the world to come than in their successful destiny in the world that is here on earth. The elder Dreiser came to America in 1844, apparently to escape military service in Germany. He was a weaver. In his westward course, he met and married a young Moravian farm girl in Pennsylvania; the marriage was against the wishes of her parents. The young couple went to Indiana and to a tragic life. Theirs was a much harassed household. They never did get settled and gain respectability and acceptance, and their usual position seems to have been that of family living, as it were, on the edge of the town—which, in fact, they often did. After John Paul Dreiser had acquired his own mill, it burned down. All the flour of the farmers in the surrounding area was inside the sheds of the mill; there was no insurance. The elder Dreiser assumed responsibility for the loss, and carried the double burden of repaying all who had suffered financial loss from the fire as well as the support of his family. Then another accident occurred. The Dreiser father was gravely injured by a beam which fell on his head and shoulders, destroying the hearing in one ear and causing a brain illness which seems to have lasted for some years at least. The first three children born to the couple all died. By the time Theodore was born, his father was practically a broken man. He emerges, in Dreiser's books, as a strict, pathetic, ineffective, rigidly religious man. Dreiser does not seem to have liked him at all. But I am inclined to believe that John Paul Dreiser set an example of moral rectitude which well might have influenced the development of that loyalty to truth which we find in his son's writings. I more than suspect that the father's example, at least unconsciously, left a valuable residue in the character of Theodore Dreiser.

Dreiser's mother was apparently a simple, unlettered woman, overburdened with cares, responsibilities and children; but she seems to have had an open, emotional nature, one which had a most powerful lifelong influence on her son Theodore. He has clearly and warmly revealed this in passages which he wrote about her, after she had long been dead. Dreiser's portrait of his mother was full, and is a living characterization rather than a sketch drawn from the recollections stamped with the distance of time that removes us from what we remember out of our yesterdays. We read about her as a woman in her completeness, not only as a mother of a large family that is much bedeviled in a nineteenth-century Indiana vale of tears.

Theodore's oldest brother was a well-known song-writer, Paul Dresser. One of his songs, which is still popular, although many do not know that Theodore Dreiser's brother wrote it, is "Frivolous Sal."

Dreiser told the story of his boyhood and early adolescent years in *Dawn,* one of the most remarkable autobiographical works that I have ever read. Dreiser's veracity enabled him to turn personal honesty into public and objectified truth. Without this volume, which I regard as one of his

[27]

finest works, we should be the losers.

He was a sensitive boy, responsive to nature. His was a feeling for beauty which, as he grew to manhood, came to be represented in the image of lovely women as well as in nature. In *Dawn* he tells of taking "long, solitary walks" accompanied by a shaggy dog, Snap. He felt a great "aloneness," and to him "the earth, its surface nature, was then truly a fairyland ...." The clouds, the sunrise, flowers, spiderwebs, "all the wonders of the morning," he felt his senses in them. He was fascinated by insects, clouds, birds, all aspects of nature. "The sudden upward rush of a meadow lark; birds' nests in the bushes or trees—these were enough to suffuse me with a rich emotional mood, tremulous, thrilling."

The Dreiser household was at least partly bilingual. In his softer moods, the elder Dreiser sang German lullabies to the children. Also, the first primary school that Theodore Dreiser attended was a German-speaking parochial institution; he hated it. The bilingual factor in his early life was no doubt an influential one in the development of Dreiser's style, and the source of critical charges of an awkwardness in the construction of many of his sentences. At school, he was an interested or an indifferent pupil, depending on his teachers; whenever one took an interest in him, he would respond. Not only in grammar school, but all through his life, and most especially in his adolescent and post-adolescent years, Dreiser learned more from life than from books or formal schooling. He learned by sensing and absorbing, by brooding, pondering and wondering, by drawing the feel of life into himself. His childhood years in Indiana, with the moving to various places, and his experiencing of towns and country, were often unhappy, but unhappiness is secondary to the fact that he was learning so much of life by the very living of it. Thus, he was gradually saturating himself with meaningful details.

One of the remarkable facts about *Dawn* is the fullness with which he was able to re-create the scenes of his childhood, the plenitude of details, including psychological ones—the memories of feeling, of thoughts, of fears and dreams, of his shyness. And he described his desires, his passions for girls; once he had reached the age of puberty, they attracted him to a degree that was torment.

And he also told of his first trip to Chicago:

"The city of which I am now about to write never was on land or sea.... The city of which I sing was not of land or sea of any time or place .... I can scarcely find it in my own soul now."

It was against a background of experience in small towns and rural nature and many people that Dreiser, stricken for life with curiousity and the wonder of everything in the world, first went to Chicago. To the new and raw city in the making he carried that same curiousity and wonder.

In time, Dreiser came to write and to express his feelings of curiousity and wonder, as well as those of pity and compassion. He created stories of the spectacle of grandeur and misery, of success and failure, which were saturated with the growing and changing America of the days and years that he knew.

II

Dreiser was a great man. It is the fact of his greatness that should make comprehensible his survival as an artist, and as one of the very few writers in the entire history of this nation who became a world figure, and who did not fade in world reputation after his death. He had more weaknesses than many talented writers can bear and carry down that lonely road that the genuine writer must traverse. All this was obvious to H.L. Mencken, who was Dreiser's champion, and who was considerably responsible for the fact that Dreiser won a hearing in America. In a letter to me, in 1943, Mencken wrote: "Dreiser, without doubt, is one of the worst writers seen on earth. Nevertheless, he has something that is hard to match . . . . "

And to Dreiser's widow, he stated in a letter: " . . . Dreiser at his best . . . was incomparable . . . . "

With every "weakness" that Mencken believed to exist in Dreiser taken into account, he nevertheless regarded Dreiser as a great man. In Dreiser, of course, the same words follow one another in his various books; there are the same names, the same moods, the same slow, sometimes lumbering sentences, the expression of a spirit that carried within itself a brooding awareness of the "essential tragedy of life." And there is the careless use of words in so many places, the lack of inventiveness—there are all of the virtues and faults, if one will, which are so characteristic of Dreiser that they could almost be termed a literary trademark, but Dreiser's virtues, his courage, his power and influence were most important in my own career, and in the careers of many others, of some like the late Richard Wright, who was younger than I, and of older writers, Hemingway and Fitzgerald, Sinclair Lewis and Sherwood Anderson.

It is the effect that counts, and the effect of Dreiser is not that of a bad writer. One does not forget his work. For instance, the decline of Hurstwood in *Sister Carrie* is unforgettable. The lack of sentimentality is but one of the remarkable features of Dreiser's account of the man's disintegration. The slow degeneration of will in Hurstwood seems to me to be a consequence of the fact that he spent his passion and the energy of his ambition on the flight with Carrie from Chicago. He was too small a fish to swim in the big ocean of New York. Although the writing moves rapidly as you read, the decomposition of inner self seems to be painfully slow. If a soul could be ashes, the soul of Hurstwood would have become such. When finally he commits suicide, he is merely confirming the fact that he has exhausted all the fundamental traits which constitute himself.

The writings of Theodore Dreiser did not come easily to him, no more than do the creations of any artist. In a letter to me of November 5, 1943, printed in full in this collection, Dreiser wrote a simple sentence: "Writing, as is, is hard enough."

Writing is hard. It is not only hard to shape into words the truth of thought and emotion as one sees them and feels them, and to endow this shaping with the best expression within one's capacity. It is also hard on the psyche, the spirit, the inner being of the artist. Every sorrow and tragedy, every joy and aspiration that a writer gives expression to is paid for; he lives them and feels them in his own psyche.

The seriousness of what we mean by fate, by destiny, is to be encountered and felt in the work of Theodore Dreiser. It is not the mere reality of a world where the flesh is weak, but where the flesh is imperious. It is not the flouting of any convention which explains the strength and (I am convinced) the lasting greatness of Dreiser's writings. Reality in his work is part of a movement, of a succession of changes, and people are engulfed in this movement, and in these changes, so that they are going onward to the point where we can see that theirs has been a fate, a destiny, career of living in time. Here is a real sense of his appeal, and, hence, of his force. To him there is—rather than victory or defeat, success or failure—mystery, the mystery of man's beginning, of his living, of his end. It is the mystery of the road that man has traversed—this is the quality of reality which Dreiser was able to embody in his writings. This is, as I see him, one of the main reasons why he can be termed a great and lasting writer of world significance.

And also, here is why you will find in this volume the poem of a mood, "The Road I Came." At the funeral services for Dreiser, held in Los Angeles, California, after his death on December 28, 1945, his friend Charles Chaplin read this poem. It suggests the quality of moody feeling

and questioning, emotionally colored thought, with which Dreiser informed his writing. There was a functional correlation between the man and his
life, and his work. This road he came filled him with awe and a ceaseless
wonder about life. It too was infused into his work. It was the source of a
curiousity which helped to motivate his writing. That writing, in turn, reflects back upon Dreiser himself, on his life.

Theodore Dreiser took his own experience seriously. He gave a value
to it. He saw it as truthfully as he could, and when he drew from it in his
books, he wrote the truth as he knew it, and wrote it as fully as he was able
to.

But this was done with an overtone of brooding, an overtone of seemingly universal brooding. He charged with emotion the questions about
man's fate. What? Why? Where to? Whence? The final meaning of the truth,
then, as he registered it in the stories of the characters he fashioned, and in
his other writing—for instance in his essay, *Hey Rub-A-Dub-Dub,* included
in this collection—is a question of mystery and the emotions which mystery evokes generally, and which are characterized by the terms *awe* and
wonder. At times, it seems as though Dreiser's evocation of these emotions
relates to man in the spaces of the universe. Dreiser was a mystic as well as
a realist, Sometimes one can find, in his pages, the shaping of a near-chaos
of life into an order which is pervaded with the tragic depth of human dignity. To achieve this impression, he had to write from a standpoint of "beyond good and evil," and not with the contempt of second-hand self-righteousness.

III

There was much unhappiness in Dreiser's boyhood, not only in young
Teddy's (the family called him "Dorsch") immediate experience, but in
that of the family generally. However, unhappiness is relative in content,
cause, extent and in depth of penetration into the psyche. Unhappiness in
human beings generally, and perhaps especially in their childhood years, is
so variable that there is no equating of it, no classification, or statistical
computation which provides understanding.

In considering unhappiness, a question which can lead to understanding is this:

What is done with unhappiness?

I have used the preposition "with" rather than "about," because
there is a distinction of perhaps profound importance to be made in refer-

ence to unhappiness; and, furthermore, this distinction needs to be applied not only to Theodore Dreiser, but fairly generally in the field of literature and pseudo-literature. I doubt that any great philosopher or other wise man would ever call man a "happy animal." But frequently, writers are called upon to do in characterization that which the wisest of men refrain from saying—make man a happy animal—which is to do something *about* unhappiness. To do something *with* unhappiness is to meet it as it occurs, and to use it for one's purposes. This is what Dreiser did in his writing. But in addition, he did something with his own unhappiness in life. He wrote of it, directly, or in the transmuted, projected form of fiction. In order to have done thus, he had to do something prior in his own life, do something directly with his own unhappiness. And here, I believe, is one of the sources of his brooding, his pondering, his slow, reflective moods and his moodiness which was evident not only to others, but to the man himself. There should be no doubt that unhappiness is a function of sensibility and awareness. When we do not consciously sense or, in relationships, are not aware of the objects of our sensibility which are not immediately present, it is obvious that we cannot be unhappy.

Dreiser did not find a world that was all right, that was all well with itself. It was not one that offered the easy escape of a dream of false happiness. But he saw beauty and wonder, as well as misery. This one can sense in his accounts of his boyhood. And he did find great hope, too, when he went to Chicago in his early teens and felt that the new city, bursting through its growth, was singing, and that he was singing with it. But throughout all this, there was in him a surge of emotions and feelings. His inner life became more wide during his early years, when he was growing up in Indiana towns and in Chicago, the new metropolis of the prairies. The world was bigger than the Midwest which Dreiser knew in the last decades of the nineteenth century. He seemed to be going nowhere; yet that was only seeming. For he was slowly beginning to find, and to *feel,* that bigness of the world. Something that need not yet happen was happening. The raw, young person, a child of a family that had failed to find the American Dream, was slowly absorbing the reality out of which was to be fashioned his own dream.

This book has been conceived as a Dreiser Reader both for those who know and for those who do not know Dreiser's work. It contains selections to reveal something of the boy, the youth, the man, of his thoughts and feelings, of the changing outer and inner world that he knew, and of a few of the creations which he fashioned out of these. Dreiser's living was a preparation for the writing of those novels which struck America with the pain of truth and the wonder of truth. I hope that this collection will lead readers on to find that *Sister Carrie* and the other major works of Dreiser are not merely novels to pick up and put down, but that they are the voice of a man who walked his own road, and who saw much, who pondered much, who brooded much, and who spoke with awe and respect of traveling that road of life which is so short, so accompanied with pain.

Here, then, is Theodore Dreiser, mystic and realist. In presenting him, I have tried to give enough of the man, his world and his creations to provide readers with a preparatory familiarity, an easier capacity for absorption in his great works, which have become part of the literature, and thus part of the memory, of the world.

1962

Writers of the Thirties

Before I can write about the writers of the thirties, I must write about the thirties.

The fourth decade of the twentieth century, the 1930s, is within living memory. I recall the very first day; it was gray, raw, and chilly. The ten years ushered in by this day are too recent for there to be such widespread misinformation and ignorance about them. They are part of an epoch and a century. They cannot be blocked off from the years that came before them and the years that came after. There is no closet of history into which man can toss time and hide it.

The thirties have more than a chronological beginning and ending. The Great Depresssion began in the fall of 1929; the year 1930 opened in depression. The Second World War began in September 1939; and the thirties ended with a world at war. There is always a "Before" and an "After." The 1930s were both.

It is a mistake to assume that the present is more subtle and complex than the past; or that it is superior as represented by those who can relate to this assumedly more subtle present. Subtlety and complexity are not assumptions that one should begin with; they are not values in themselves. Nor are they virtues.

Much of the thinking of the thirties was related to the experience of the First World War and its aftermath—the postwar disillusionment that was felt in the 1920s. This postwar disillusionment represented the failure of many ideals; but it was more than the failure of ideals; it was the failure of men—the failure of leaders.

Advanced nations could not avert a war. And once begun, a war could not be stopped. The glory and glamour of war were turned into seeds of bitter disillusionment. Very few had envisioned a long war but the fighting and bloodshed went on for more than four years.

In Paris, an outburst of patriotism brought crowds into the streets, mobs shouting "On to Berlin."

And in Berlin, the crowds shouted: "On to Paris."

The majority of the Socialist leaders stood for the defense of the country. The resolutions of the Basle Congress of 1908 gave way to a pro-war position. The intellectuals came out strongly in patriotic support of their own countries.

Thus, a world was shattered. A world of ideals, an ideological world, a world of the meaning of life and of lives for ages—all this had led to a war of inglorious mud and blood that could not be stopped. The sense of use-lessness, of hideous, bleeding, rotting corpses strewn widely over shell-rav-aged fields, the wounded and murdered spent to capture yonder mile or half-mile of trench, helpless men lying in mud with their final fate beyond their power.

The thinking and feeling of many became a matter of shattered cer-tainties. Progress was suspect. Western Man with all his hopes and dreams had come to a bloody impasse. (It is only the instinctive health of man that has kept him from knowing too fully how sick at heart he has been for decades.) After the world had been suffering blood, relief was wildness.

The prelude to the twenties was the spontaneous eruptions of the Armistice Day celebrations.

Then the Peace of Versailles, the League of Nations (called a "Thieves' Kitchen" by Lenin). It was repudiated by the American Senate and by the American people. From its inception, it was fated to fail. It was founded in the quicksands of a temporary correlation of superior pow-ers in command and control.

America emerged from the First World War an undamaged, victorious nation with tremendous wealth and economic power. Americans became aware of this power, of their new position and prestige. In the 1920 Amer-ican presidential election, the candidate selected in a smoke-filled hotel room, Warren Harding, spoke of carrying on a front porch campaign. From misuse of language, he coined a new word. He proposed that we get "back to normalcy." "Back to Normalcy" became the impossible hope. Wood-row Wilson, sick in the White House, had been repudiated not by a "little group of willful men," not by a group of isolationist senators, but by his own people. He had collapsed on a speaking tour which he had heroically undertaken to defend the Treaty of Versailles and the League of Nations.

Absurb conclusions were drawn in the twenties. The American Standard of Living and the American Way of Life were impregnable. These years were tagged the "roaring twenties."

They were also the "speculating twenties." Money is not subjected to monetary birth control. It has to beget more and more and more money. But things economic can't be that way. Why? They just can't be.

Men are not personified money. Some men act as though they were. And so there were booms and more booms and still more booms. Where could the most be gotten from an invested dollar? Men, as personified money, rushed after higher rates of profits, quicker turnover. Correspondingly, a quicker and faster return, plus profit, of the invested dollar. This was a feature of the 1920s which permitted the lambs to lie down with the wolves; and the lambs were well-fleeced.

The twenties were an energetic decade. America was spilling over with energy. There were changes in every corner. A few million Americans had been soldiers, some heroes. There had been many examples of violence. "The revolt of youth" was a phrase often used.

Then there were changes, important changes, based on technological advances. New industries, types of organizations, methods of distribution and dissemination entered these fields of endeavor. The Book-of-the-Month Club was founded. The Theater Guild came into being. New publishing houses went into business, applying advertising methods that made best sellers.

However, these developments and manifestations were only part of a broader change that was fundamentally economic. This was the explanation of the consumer market. A pronounced shift toward a consumption attitude is evident during this period. This included an increased audience for various cultural productions. And there was bigness. This bigness was even a feature of gangsterism and bootlegging.

The so-called law of supply and demand was relied upon to keep the American market functioning with economic health. But the demand for speculative profit outdistanced other demands. Values became inflated beyond any economic reason. The boom became a bust. America found herself falling into the Great Depression.

By January 1, 1930, millions were out of work and they could not find that corner, around which many business and political leaders claimed that prosperity was waiting to be regained.

There were, of course, varying reactions to the trends of events and the quick rise of mass unemployment. Misery mounted and spread but there was only partial awareness of this. There were many who believed that the unemployed were at fault and commented on suffering and hunger with platitudes of "rugged individualism" and commonplace vulgarizations taken from the Social Darwinism of the late 1800s. From high places, there were comments that just about all that was needed was for the American businessman to get his tail feathers off the ground and the essential soundness of the American economy would be restored. This optimism was based on the assumption that the infallible working laws of economics could be set right. It was believed that if the best men, a sort of consortium of best men, got together, they could get things going again by reviving those laws of economy, especially that of supply and demand. Further, they believed that this effort should begin at the top and that interventions should be channeled to the top. This was essentially the thinking of President Hoover's Reconstruction Finance Corporation Policy. Loans to the railroads and to the big fellows generally would cause a business pick-up; there would be a trickling down of benefits. To this day, these ideas are held by many top businessmen. And we are still in danger of having the actual test of events made of these ideas. Our economic system has been far less modified since 1930 than is believed. Bigness has gotten bigger.

Bigness existed right on through the thirties. A number of New Deal reforms were long overdue. In the main, the first stage of New Deal reforms enabled the United States, more or less, to catch up with the so-called socialist laws of Chancellor Otto von Bismarck of the First Reich back in the 1870s.

During the first three years of the thirties, there were waves of misery and resentment spreading across America. Farmers were in a near-rebellion. Foreclosures on mortgaged farms were common. Farmers got out shotguns to protect their homes. They went to auctions armed, determined to prevent the sale of seized farmlands.

In Detroit, the unemployed had ice cold water shot upon them when they gathered at a Ford plant to seek jobs. In March of 1930, unemployed demonstrations were organized by the Communist Party, U.S.A., in New York and in Chicago. Before these demonstrations, the police of both cities had broken up meetings with clubs. Protests were made by liberals and others and the result was that the huge demonstrations were policed and peaceable.

There was the Hunger March on Washington. The Bonus March. The Bonus Marchers were driven out of Anacousta Flats in Washington by regular army troops.

The pattern of violence which had manifested itself in the twenties with gangland wars continued into the thirties. But there was a new atmosphere of violence developing. It was a violence born of a depression and of strikes and demonstrations.

There is a definite relationship of writers to their time. The role of writers varies in accordance with the times and the character of the society in which they live. It is extremely difficult for a writer to play an independent role here in America. To say what role a writer performs is to ask what function is fulfilled by his work. The printed word is an influence, often a powerful one. In the long term of history, it has been the most powerful. But in America, it did not seem to be so. Writing did not seem a potent factor in the progress that was believed to be taking place to a greater extent and more rapidly than was actually the fact.

1962
(fragment)

On Zola

The final lines of Emile Zola's *Germinal* can help explain the spirit of his writing:

Men were springing forth, a black avenging army, germinating slowly in the furrows, growing towards the harvests of the next century, and this germinating would soon overturn the earth.

Above all else, germination in Zola's work and thought meant the triumph of the truth. It was after all Zola who proudly proclaimed, in the face of the French General Staff, that "the Truth is on the march."

No great novelist of the last hundred years has been more savagely denounced and attacked than is Zola. And a few great novelists of this period have had a more pervasive influence than he. Zola was an audacious innovator. He developed theories concerning the creation of what he called the experimental novel. By this he meant the scientific novel. He claimed that the novelist must and could be a scientist. Here I shall not, however, go into detail concerning these theories. A number of specific objections can be made to them. But his central purpose can be simply phrased. The novelist should seek the truth, and when he finds it, he should not soften its impact with polite circumlocutions. And Zola was attacked because this is precisely what he tried to do in his novels. Literary critics have now blasted these novels for decades. Even at the present time, there are many critics who use his very name as a term of denunciation. If such critics can associate a contemporary writer with Zola's name, they then will read that writer out of the very domain of literature. In Zola's own lifetime, the attacks were stronger than they are now. When *Nana* first appeared in England, the publisher was indicted for allegedly publishing obscene literature. A vicious press campaign was carried on by the defenders of drawing room hypocrisy. The publisher was driven into bankruptcy. The English publication of Zola was stopped. But his influence was not halted. Zola, as Havelock Ellis observed, contributed towards broadening and liberating literature in England. The same is true in America. His work served as an example for earlier American realists. He exerted a strong influence on Frank Norris. He stands behind Dreiser. Havelock Ellis also, and justly, described his bold innovations as heroic. And writing in *The Atlantic Monthly*, August 1903, Henry James referred to "the circumstances that, thirty years ago, a young man of extraordinary brain and indomitable purpose, wishing to give the measure of these endowments in a piece of work supremely solid, conceived and set down to *Les Rougon-Macquart,* rather than to an equal task in physics, mathematics, politics, economics. He saw his undertaking, thanks to his patience and courage, practically to a close . . . . No finer act of courage and confidence, I think, is recorded in the history of letters. The critic in sympathy with him returns again and again to the great wonder of it, in which something so strange is mixed with something so august. Entertained and carried out almost from the threshold of manhood, the high project, the work of a lifetime, announces beforehand its inevitable weakness, and yet speaks in the same voice for its admirable, its almost unimaginable, strength." Henry James' observations are especially significant today because James' own work—so different from that of Zola—is used again and again by genteel critics in their effort to destroy the influence of any writer whom they can associate with the tendencies exemplified in Zola's writing.

Zola's novel *Nana* is perhaps the most widely read of his books at the present time. It is available both in the Modern Library and in a twenty-five-cent reprint edition, and seems to be the only Zola novel now enjoying a general circulation in America. *Nana* is the story of a French courtesan during the period of the Second Empire. She was modelled after the famous courtesans, singers and actresses of that day. In collecting information for this novel, Zola went to Hortense Schneider, Zulma Bouffar and others who, in our language, would be called the glamour girls of the era of Offenbach and of Louis Napoleon.

Nana's childhood is described in Zola's great novel of disintegration, *L'Assommoir.* Her mother was a laundress who walked with a slight limp.

Her father was a good workman until he sustained an injury which incapacitated him for a long period. Then he changed. He became lazy, and gradually fell to drinking. He brought a former lover of the mother's into the household, and in fact, gave the mother away to this lover. The mother, in time, abandoned her efforts to hold the family together and to develop her small laundry business. She, along with the father, disintegrated. Her first steps towards disintegration were revealed in overeating and in a growing obesity. Of the mother, Zola observed that she no longer had "the strength to be frightened when she thought of the future." In his descriptions of Nana as a child, Zola reveals her as vicious. She is up to all sorts of tricks. She delights in seeing her father and mother abuse one another. She watches her parents, and also her mother and a lover, in intimate relationships. When Nana's grandmother dies, Nana immediately gets into the bed of the deceased, and enjoys its comfort without a thought of the old woman who had only just died. Nana becomes a flower girl. On Sundays, she roams the streets of Paris, flirting as do the other girls of her neighborhood. If her father catches her, he beats her. All of her traits are indicated in miniature in Zola's account of her childhood. In a surprising way, she acquires the wasteful and demoralizing traits of her parents, both of whom end up as insane and derelict alcoholics. I have made these observations here because on making a comparison between Nana, and her parents, and on noting Nana's traits as a child, I have come to the conclusion that critics have done Zola an injustice. There is more psychological insight in his books than readers might be immediately aware of. This is revealed in the way in which he shows how Nana evolves and develops a character which is a new combination of the traits and habits of her parents. Formally, of course, Zola attributes this to hereditary influences. But regardless of any such general explanation, there is an amazing consistency in the characterization of Nana.

As I have already suggested, the contemporary phrase for Nana is "glamour girl." At the opening of the novel named for her, she is appearing in a light opera, playing the role of Venus. She is extraordinarily attractive to men. The producer of the opera says: "Does a woman need to know how to dance and sing? My boy, you're stupid . . . Nana has something else, by Heaven! And something that is better than all the rest. I have noticed it in her; she has it strongly . . . She has only to show herself and she'll make their mouths water."

Nana succeeds on the stage purely because of her sex appeal. In passing, the opera, as described by Zola, suggests Offenbach, a man whom

Zola was to criticize sharply. As a consequence of her success, Nana becomes the talk of luxury-loving Paris. Almost overnight, she becomes a famous courtesan. She takes the paramours of other courtesans away from them. She is supported in luxury. She is wasteful, immoral, irresponsible, childish. Luxury and success do not touch her. In the midst of her fame and glory, she abandons her career to live with an ugly actor. She reverts to her childhood, and to the pattern of her mother. She accepts beatings and even takes to the streets and descends to the lower depths of Parisian life in order to feed the actor whom she loves. Only when he locks her out does she rise again!

When Nana comes back, she becomes a devourer of men. They are ruined financially by her luxuries. She wastes hundreds of thousands of francs a year. She is impelled to destroy. And with this, we see her as infantile, narcissistic, completely self-centered. She has childish fears of death, and becomes utterly terrified by fears of hell fire. Then, she plunges once again into her life of pleasure.

Zola is often regarded as a literal and photographic realist. His effects are achieved by an almost monumental piling on of facts and details. He was strongly opposed to the romantic writers who preceded him, and *Nana*, at times, reads almost like an anti-romantic tract. And yet at the same time, Nana becomes a romantic symbol in reverse, of a negative order. She is an elemental force. In the last analysis, the themes of Zola's books were forces rather than characters. Energy, power, the working out of the laws of heredity and environment as these were seen scientifically in Zola's day—these are almost the real protagonists of his work. His characters are personifications of these forces and these laws. Just as in *Germinal* the mind is like an elemental force devouring men, so is Nana an elemental force, devouring and destroying. All of the settings of her life are romantic. Her love affairs, her very home have an almost operatic character. The vicious little raggedy girl of the Parisian gutters develops into the all-punishing and even monstrous courtesan. Men commit suicide. Homes are wrecked. High officials in the Tuilleries destroy their careers for her. This mounts in a crescendo of madness. And then, Nana disappears.

There are many rumors about her. She is often talked of. But suddenly she returns to Paris. But she has come back ill, and with smallpox. As she lies dying, there are crowds on the boulevards outside, shouting, marching, crying out again and again:

"On to Berlin! On to Berlin!"

Nana's death occurs on the day that the Franco-Prussian war begins. The shouting crowds, led by workingmen in blouses, introduce a new elemental force. Nana, representing a devouring and elemental force of sex, dies, and war comes, preparing for a debacle.

1966

George Ade:
Creator of "Artie" and "Pink Marsh"

George Ade remains a writer of the first order. His influence upon the literature of the twentieth century is strong and, unfortunately, not always apparent. He was close to Peter Finley Dunne, whom he knew. As Dunne was a great writer, Ade was next door to greatness, and at moments he too achieved greatness. He should be lasting; he was a masterful short-story writer, surpassing O. Henry. I dislike making these comparisons, lifting up one writer at the expense of another, but here there is reason for my doing what normally I condemn.

O. Henry stirs pity for the struggle there was in his life, but in his writings there is often something that does not ring genuine. Too, there is a carefree twisting of everything into the picturesque. It is all largely verbal, a play on sentiment. The "trick ending," the "snapper" that surprises, cancels sincere feeling and the creation of a sense of realness.

Ade was natural, and his characterizations promptly take on reality. He refuses to trick his situations or trademark his endings. They are as natural as the events reported in the newspaper for which he wrote. He called himself a realist, and he qualifies. He began with people, not situations. His realism was a consequence of his interest in people and the talent he had for making them come alive in what he wrote.

Ade was born in 1866, in Kentland, Indiana, a small town about eighty miles from Chicago. The surrounding area was farmland. Ade, as he grew up, turned out not to possess the qualities that make a farmer; but as a boy he was a good listener, and he learned to make more than hay out of what city slickers might consider hayseed talk. Ade listened to endless talk, and he heard dialogue, dialogue about the weather and other subjects that are the common currency of people who have nothing to say to each other. He heard the humor of it. The early Hoosier days were the source of his flavorful language and the originality in its use that became George Ade's contribution to American literature—the use of language "as it is spoke" in his short stories and fables.

He started as a newspaper writer. Day after day he wrote his "Fables in Slang"; and day after day he had fresh subjects, he did not repeat himself. His ironic touches, his alert regard for the twists and turns of fate, his good-natured humor, and—it needs to be said—his sometimes Philistine smugness. Yes, these are some of the traits and qualities found in the writings of George Ade.

He had an ear, an eye, and a ranging curiosity about people and their destinies.

Here are two early volumes by George Ade: *Artie,* which was originally published in 1896, and *Pink Marsh,* first issued in book form in 1897. By that time Ade could consider himself a success. He had attracted the notice, among others, of William Dean Howells and Hamlin Garland. But before he reached Chicago at the age of twenty-four, he graduated from college and tried reading law, and then he got a job as a journalist on a newly founded newspaper in Lafayette, Indiana. The newspaper was *The Call,* and Ade's salary was $8 a week. Next he got a job selling patent medicines for a company that promptly failed. And off he went to Chicago to join his college classmate and lifelong friend, John T. McCutcheon, who was at the station to meet him and took him along to the hall bedroom they were to share. George Ade's half of the rent was to be $2.50, and to afford it he had to have a job. He was promptly hired by the *Morning News,* to do a daily piece on the weather.

To coin a banality, it seemed an inauspicious beginning. And it would have been so for almost anyone by George Ade. He was older than the pluck-and-luck boys of Horatio Alger Jr.'s imagination, but he had something better than a shoeshine box to help him make the most of opportunity. He had George Ade. And George Ade could make even the weather seem interesting.

Soon he began to do general reporting, and his pay was raised to $15 a week. He did legwork, going out on all kinds of stories. He came to know Chicago "like a laboratory." This experience prepared him for the writing he was to do. He saw much more of Chicago than a reporter is likely to see today. He saw it purely and simply. He had lived close to the farm, in a small town. Everywhere there were sharp contrasts to be seen.

In almost all of the earlier writings about Chicago that have retained their significance, the writers had this advantage of perceiving in contrasts. They came to Chicago as to something new. The very coming to Chicago was a story, or a part of a story. It was even more—it was an adventure, a change of life. Chicago was new, a city of many hopes, the locale of adventure. It was new not only to writers and aspiring writers, but to thousands and thousands of people. In a sense, Chicago was new to itself. Dreiser had his own sense of Chicago as new, and he saw the rising inland metropolis as a Venice of dreams. Ade was the greater realist. He was realistic about people and their patterns of behavior, and he was less likely to be upset by their foibles and their blindnesses.

Artie and *Pink Marsh* can be classified as novels. Each consists of a series of episodes taken from Ade's newspaper columns. Ade chose only the best of the pieces about Artie and Pink Marsh and their encounters and experiences in and about Chicago. And from these random pieces we can feel emerge Ade's sense of character.

For the creation of Artie Blanchard he drew literally on a boy who worked in the art department of his newspaper. Ade's biographer, Fred Kelly, quotes the boy:

"I didn't do a thing but push my face in there [a church entertainment] about eight o'clock last night, as I was 'it' from the start. Say, I like that church and if they'll put in a punchin' bag and a plunge, they can have my game, I'll tell you those."

Ade used this verbatim in *Artie*. Most writers do something like this, but first there is invention, the use of the imagination, the creation of character and event in sequence, the establishment of the illusion of reality— even the choice of where and how the verbatim quotations are to be used. Life itself is the model for writers, always—even if it be a pattern of fantasy and dream that violates the laws of the external universe.

Artie works in a business office, not a newspaper office. He goes about as much as he can, and he tells his experiences to Miller, who is older and rather sedate. Miller does not know what the city is like after working hours. In telling his experiences, Artie grows. He falls in love, and we find him love-struck and moony and younger than he thinks himself to be. Here Ade seems to have had just the right amount of restraint. Ade never laughs at Artie or spills over into sentimentality. This is the way it should be in all good and true fiction. Ade does not need to depend upon suspense to maintain interest in his characters. He does not make them toe a story-line. Again, the characters are the story.

Artie is a natural characterization, with no false or forced caricature. There is no easy evasion by exaggeration, no grotesque clichés on the slapstick level. George Ade gives Artie the simplicity of his human proportions, thus making Artie touchingly real.

Pink Marsh is a Negro shoeshine boy, working in a barber shop one flight down. Like Artie, Pink Marsh confides in someone older than himself, in this case the "morning customer," who likes him, is amused by him, and sometimes offers advice and encouragement.

The use of dialect, phonetically rendered, is not practiced much today. There is less need of it now than there was when George Ade wrote *Pink Marsh.* At that time differences in speech and accent stood out in a very pronounced way.

In the 1890s, differences in behavior, dress, manner and manners, were striking. These were the bubbles to be seen on the surface of the American melting pot. Differences in speech quickly aroused the interest of many. Ade, who had listened to farm folk in Indiana, took the same interest in the prototypes of Artie and Pink Marsh. These were "new voices" to him. He listened and transcribed. This was a new generation of Americans, who saw a Chicago he would not have seen without their eyes. They were not hod-carriers, teamsters, bricklayers, ditchdiggers, and they were not foreigners. They went to work dressed up, and they expected to rise in the world. They had gone to school—at least to grammar school. Living in the big city, they had lost some of their small-town mores. Some were salesmen, able to travel about in the course of their work. They were beginning to think they knew what for the world is round.

They felt their sense of difference from the mass, the great unwashed, as a quality of their own self-esteem. (This is true of both Artie and Pink Marsh, though neither expresses it directly.) They were very conscious of differences. In a city the size of Chicago differences exist.

Ade pleased them by so carefully reproducing the talk of the "darky," the Irishman with his brogue, the expostulating Italian; and, in a number of instances, the hick or rube who was thought to have straw in his ears and was quick to defend the virtues of the farm and prove his own sagacity.

Other factors were involved in the development of interest in slang and the vernacular. It seemed to express the wonder and reality of city life, of so much that was a part of the world. It had no connection with the twice-removed air of the language in books. Many, of course, had no other command of the language as a means of expression. In Chicago, in particular, it was becoming an electrically alive current in city life. It expressed so much that had not been thought or said.

Pink Marsh, as well as *Artie,* needs to be regarded in a certain perspective, and I have suggested some of the factors which ought to be considered in reading these sketches.

The use of phonetic spelling to catch the sound of living speech was a virtual necessity at the time Ade was creating *Pink Marsh.* Speech in the places of work and of commerce, on street corners, in barber shops, in saloons, in offices, and on front stoops was rich in variety and full of the pathos of differences. And George Ade had learned to express them all without drowning the amusing.

At the time Ade was writing this was so common and so widespread, manifest daily, that it became an unavoidable element in popular writing. Mark Twain began it, and after him came George Ade and Peter Finley Dunne. Ring Lardner followed; his successor, I suppose, is Salinger. And I've not mentioned Stephen Crane, whose *Maggie, a Girl of the Streets* contains a phonetic rendering of the voluble discourse of uneducated people.

Pink Marsh is also a forerunner. Pink was living before the racial strain in Chicago became menacing. Pink, of course, serves white men. He is not only unusually talkative, unrestrained, and expressive, but he has an inner core of dignity which sets him apart from the caricatures of Octavus Roy Cohen, of a later date. (I have in mind Florian Slappey, Cohen's chief character.)

The significance of dialect and how it is rendered is forgotten today. It was a means of revealing character, background, social roles, and relationships. Of course, when I imply the terms sociological and psychological I am differentiating only for purposes of emphasis. Human beings are not aggregations of categories, classes, facts, data, and types.

George Ade was criticized because he chose to step down into a barber shop and write about the people he found there. But it is wise to suspect that Ade found Pink and his like more interesting than those Pink served.

Pink describes to the "morning customer" the happenings in which he is involved. These occur among the colored population of the South Side, and they include a good number of accounts of Pink's own experiences with the girls he likes and the men who are his rivals. From chapter to chapter, day to day, Pink grows in a kind of rich, comic reality. Unlike Artie, he is sometimes allowed to be the wise fool. There is much shrewdness in Pink's make-up, underneath the ill-education; and in the same way Artie, who is wise beyond his years, is shown to have a core of naïveté. In both Pink and Artie there is much of Ade's own venturing personality. By endowing Pink and Artie with his own characteristics, George Ade saves them from stereotype. Artie is both knowing and tender; Pink is both an "Uncle Tom" and a true-born Yankee. The gap between Pink and his customers is revealed in dialogue, but always the energy of his impressions keeps him real. Any air of patronization that the reader wishes to read into Ade's characterization of Pink is dispelled beyond doubt by the clear-eyed view Pink has of those who work in the shop or the customers who come there. Pink is shrewd, knowing, and sometimes farcical, but he has a great many of Ade's traits and characteristics. Ade could not have written about him if this were not so.

George Ade was a phenomenon, an American phenomenon. He was next door to literary greatness. He was recognized and applauded by the many who came after him. He helped to create and condition the audience now clamoring for the works of American writers.

Oscar Wilde said: "To reveal art and conceal the art is the artist's aim." In *Pink Marsh,* the story of a Negro shoeshine boy with whom George Ade obviously identifies, Ade's birthplace, his education, his experience are concealed—he creates a real character named Pink. This is the phenomenon of George Ade. And the same can be said of his championship of Artie, who is so unlike the Hoosier writer who created him.

Both novels are readable today, almost seven decades after they were written. The two books combined here are among the first in George Ade's career. His writing has a lasting brightness about it. I find that I can reread it today without losing any of the enjoyment I had in many different years of the past.

1963

The Value of
Literature in Modern Society

I would like to say first that the most important thing that a person can do is to teach. It is much more important to implant a sense of truth and a love of life in a young mind than it is to own a factory making tin cans that are five miles square. If there be no teacher, there be no future.

REMARKS ON LITERATURE AND EDUCATION

Education is simply locating yourself in life and learning how to control the processes of nature and social living. Presently the emphasis on criticism has affected many English departments. Students are asked, "What is the criticism of Anton Chekhov?" If a nineteen-year-old boy, unless he is a genius, stood up and said, "The criticism of Chekhov is . . . . " I would say to him, "Sit down. You don't know what the hell you're talking about."

Literature is not precisely a means of education; I think it should be presented to students rather than be taught to them. I am strongly against the emphasis on contemporary writing to the degree that you find it in colleges and high schools. I think they should be exposed to Dante and Milton and be given the basis, at least, of a historical sense of literature.

The most important thing that I got from my education was that I gained a sense of truth in the world. I learned that one must be loyal to truth. If I violated it, I would feel myself a criminal.

As I stated earlier, I think students should be exposed to literature;

not taught it. To those who do not read, that's it. Those who do enjoy reading gain a deep sense of what is most important of all. They see the tragic and sometimes hopeful, great, yet sad, continuity of mankind from generation to generation.

WHAT LITERATURE MEANS

A much misunderstood book is Tolstoy's *What Is Art?* I would like to quote a passage from this book which tells you very well what literature is about:

And thanks to man's capacity to express thoughts by words, every man may know all that has been done for him in the realms of thought by all humanity before his day, and can, in the present, thanks to this capacity to understand the thoughts of others, become a sharer in their activity, and can himself, as can his contemporaries, assess thoughts he has assimilated from others as well as those which have arisen within himself. So thanks to man's capacity to be infected with the feelings of others by means of art, all that is to be lived thoroughly by a contemporary is accessible to him, as well as the experience of men thousands of years ago, and there is also the possibility of transmitting his own feelings to others. If people lacked this capacity to receive a thought perceived by the men who preceded them and to pass on to others their own thoughts, men would be like wild beasts. And if men lacked the other capacity of being infected by art, people might be almost more savage still and, above all, more separated and more hostile to one another.

That quotation embodies very much the sense of what literature should mean. The most important words of what I quoted are "to be infected with feeling," because if art could not infect one with feeling, he has missed it. The same thing can be said of literature.

LITERATURE IN HISTORY

I think in high schools today students should get a feeling for the historical sense of literature. We must see literature in a historical context. In this country there is a sort of contempt for history. It has declined from what it used to be. Literature is interchangeable with the times. Great literature is always contemporary. In high schools we should read the great works of Dante, Milton, and Chekhov.

Three hundred years ago this year, Milton finished *Paradise Lost* and

Paradise Regained. The seventeenth century, the time of Milton, was a century of scientific revolution. Milton was completely oblivious to the science of his time.

The great work of the thirteenth century was Dante's *Inferno.* Though this was the concept of the future at that time, this work portrayed the medieval idea that the world is a stage on which the drama of man's salvation is played out. There is a remarkable unity, of feeling and idea, between Dante's *Inferno* and the writings of the summa-theologian Saint Thomas Acquinas.

Students should see the connection between past literature and literature of the present. We are living the kind of life that should always think of the future. In a sense the present never counts. It is the future that always counts. Without thinking of the future, we cannot think of the present or the past with any clarity. The pace of change has been so rapid that we are living with much undigested experience. We change technologically, but we do not change psychologically. A great writer, if she had lived, Frances Newman, said, "Techniques proliferate rapidly, but human emotion does not change."

The concept of continuity and change that applies to science also applies to history, society, and literature. From generation to generation we find that people see, feel, and think about things somewhat differently. One set of feelings is not better than another set of emotions. Through the years we think of writers as good and bad. We should not think of literature in terms of naturalism, realism, etc. This is a waste of time.

Literature is, perhaps, the most powerful of arts. It is a means of preserving the memory of mankind. It is a means of eulogizing one's inner life. He who tampers with the memory of mankind is a moral criminal.

Anyone who has read Dante's *Inferno, Paradise Lost, Paradise Regained, War and Peace, Madame Bovary,* and any other of the first-rate works of greatness has enlarged his inner life.

Literature is concerned with reality. It is the poet, the philosopher, and the historian who know reality and life, and it is the practical man who manipulates it. Reality is many-sided and very complicated because each thing that is seen or felt is seen or felt from each individual's psyche in a certain condition.

WHAT IS LITERATURE?

There is as much passion in writing today as there was one hundred years ago. Each story portrays human emotion and passion in its own form. An example of this is Maxim Gorky's conversation with Anton Chekhov. He tells of a hideous scene—a poor drunken old woman lying in the gutter, her frightened child standing and staring. Chekhov shuddered and shook his head and went on gently. He said, "She was so slippery and slimy I could not touch her." Tears ran down the boy's cheek. "Mommy, do get up." She'd try and she'd fall back into the gutter.

I must not write about filth. Then I said, why not write about this. I must write about everything. If everything is not written about, this little boy might be hurt. It matters what is truth.

In the quest of education, it is a matter of giving the child a sense of truth, of awakening his feeling. Alfred N. Whitehead refers to those who miseducate and distort ideas as soul murderers. He who censors a book practically kills a life.

Gorky, in a tribute to Anton Chekhov, spoke of this great writer:

Out of the gray mass of helpless people there comes a great, wise, and observant man with the tone of anguish in his heart. He said to these people, "You live badly, my friends."

I would also like to mention to those of you who may not know this: Tolstoy established a school for children; he started to write stories for children; and some of these are his best writings. I would like to advise you who are interested to read the writings about his school and particularly to read what he wrote about science, nature, and life for children. He was the kind of genius who comes about every ten centuries.

It is through art and literature that we can hope to see everyone become better by realizing more fully his or her potential as an individual, social, and human being. That is the purpose of ideas, knowledge, science, and literature. Otherwise, it is all meaningless.

1966

F. Scott Fitzgerald
and His Romanticism

When Fitzgerald's first books were published back in the twenties, they were exciting to young people. Within the blaring limits of "the jazz age," Fitzgerald presented characters and events of an upper social level which many could never reach. Fitzgerald's world was the world of the Ivy League, fraternities and sororities. There were Princeton men, Yale men, rich boys and rich girls who drank hooch, carried flasks, danced past three o'clock in the morning, or even until the daylight was about to dawn. They necked and they talked philosophical platitudes about life and love, about sex and love. They were frank with each other against a background of raccoon coats and cheers at a football game, or against a background of rouged knees and satin flapper dresses with moaning saxophones at a college dance.

Fitzgerald's first novel, *This Side of Paradise,* was published in March, 1920. He was twenty-three years old. The book was an immediate success.

Malcolm Cowley, writing in *Exile's Return* years later, wrote that *This Side of Paradise* was a "bad novel but an honest one." Granville Hicks in *The Great Tradition* thought that it "expressed the bewilderment and hopelessness of youth." Edmund Wilson, who had known Fitzgerald at Princeton, wrote him that the book "verged on the ludicrous."

But most reviewers praised Fitzgerald's first novel. Older critics seemed more enthusiastic about the book than reviewers close to Fitzgerald's age.

In *This Side of Paradise,* there is some accepted connection between the protagonist Amory Blaine and Fitzgerald. Amory Blaine is interested in reading, as was Fitzgerald. Many of Fitzgerald's friends claimed that Fitzgerald had read considerably less than he credits to himself in his first novel; but this is irrelevant. Amory Blaine is Fitzgerald's character; we must accept what Fitzgerald says that Amory has read. Amory reads many writers who are hopeful and optimistic about the future of mankind—H.G. Wells, Arnold Bennett, George Bernard Shaw, Samuel Butler. At the end of the book, Amory Blaine has presumably grown from a "Romantic Egotist" to a "Personage" and is dissatisfied and discontent with these writers. He feels that they have let him down. As a character, Amory Blaine is now drawn as a man with much capacity for judgment. There is no marked development in him, no profound awakening. And yet, in the end—even though the world is in a bit of a muddle, Amory Blaine knows himself. Amory is a romanticist. Romantic poets from Shelley to Rupert Brooke appeal to him. He loves and understands Keats, as does Fitzgerald.

The spiritual father of Romanticism was Jean Jacques Rousseau. In *The Confessions of Jean Jacques Rousseau,* we can summarize Rousseau by saying that there is a willful substitution of sensibility for sense. Rousseau broadened the range of sensibility and the area of expressed feeling. This expressed feeling in words and deeds is a special endowment that makes the romanticist unique. This is at the core of Romanticism.

Another figure of great influence in the historic development of Romanticism was Lord Byron. From Rousseau and Byron, we have Romanticism on the plane of history. In his life and in his writing, Byron was up on the level of history. Don Juan is a traditional cultural figure of a lover.

Romanticism had decayed by the time F. Scott Fitzgerald wrote of Amory Blaine, and of his successor Anthony Patch in *The Beautiful and the Damned.* Romanticism was a pose, a flood of quotations as you danced dreamily with a special girl in your arms at three o'clock in the morning, or as you participated in some college hijinks after several swigs of bootleg booze.

Romanticism had decayed. And it was this which betrayed Amory Blaine and confused his creator, F. Scott Fitzgerald.

I consider *The Great Gatsby* Fitzgerald's best written book. *The Great Gatsby* is frozen Romanticism. Gatsby is a vague character. The reason for this, I think, is that Fitzgerald created Gatsby as living out a nostalgic adolescent dream. Gatsby had loved the girl Daisy when he had been seventeen. Since then, he had amassed considerable wealth as a bootlegger. He has a house built and creates surroundings to befit a seventeen-year-old's romantic feelings.

Fitzgerald was not a writer with strength although he was a writer who had qualities. He is best describing surfaces, setting down situations, establishing locations, and adding glitter to a scene where there are a number of people. These qualities are shown well in *The Great Gatsby*.

But what of the substance of the novel?

Gatsby, as a gangster, is a romantic image of the 1920s. Early in the book, Fitzgerald wrote:

If personality is an unbroken series of successful gestures, then there was something gorgeous about him, some heightened sensitivity to the promise of life, as if he were related to one of those intricate machines that register earthquakes ten miles away.

And Fitzgerald also wrote:

(Gatsby's) responsiveness was an extraordinary gift for hope, a romantic readiness . . . .

Gatsby is all that Amory Blaine and Anthony Patch would be if they had had the capacity to be romantically gorgeous and sensitive. However, Gatsby's sensibility not his sensitivity is revealed. It is asserted; we never come upon it.

The *Great Gatsby* was published in 1925.

Tender Is the Night appeared in 1934. Legend is that this novel received sales-destroying reviews and had a poor sales. But as Andrew Turnbull points out, *Tender Is the Night* was more favorably than unfavorably reviewed. More influential literary figures hailed this book than attacked it. The book sold 13,000 copies. Fitzgerald was reported to be humiliated by such a poor sale. Actually, in 1934, the United States was still deep in the Great Depression; 13,000 was a good sale. However, good or bad, the sales neither prove nor disprove anything about the book. The author's reaction is more revealing.

F. Scott Fitzgerald regarded *Tender Is the Night* as his masterpiece. At the same time, he lacked confidence. Assurance for him depended upon the reviews, the sales. There is a pathos about this uncertainty, and a poignancy.

Here, I would like to mention Fitzgerald's short stories; some of these are truly first rate. One of these, "May Day", can be considered a great story

Many of his short stories are good and it is through these, I believe, that F. Scott Fitzgerald will live in American Literature.

1971

The Irish Cultural Renaissance in the Last Century

Nationalism—the concept of the nation—permeates all Irish thinking: it pervades Irish writing. However, one cannot interpret nationalism in Irish writing as though it were a hardened and unchanging conception. The concept of the nation, the precise character of nationalism in Irish writing, has gone through various changes in the course of the last hundred years.

In Ireland, disputes concerning propaganda and literature have been focused in terms of the national movement. In the politics of the national movement, there have been two tendencies, one which put the political question of national sovereignty first, and the other which stressed the social question. Figures representing these tendencies in the early twentieth century were Arthur Griffith, the leader who played the key role in founding Sinn Fein, and James Connolly, the national martyr and social revolutionary. The difference here can be suggested in the question—which comes first, the national or the social question?

A difference somewhat parallel can be seen when we touch on the question of literature and propaganda. Do the political interests of the national movement, narrowly conceived, come before the interests of a literature created in pursuit of an image of truth? Can literature be judged in terms of a fixed national aim so that it is turned into a political handmaiden?

Discussing these questions years ago in his book *Principles of Freedom,* the late Terence MacSwiney, an Irish martyr, declared: "It is because we need the truth that we object to the propagandist playwright." It is this idea of an image of the truth which is denied by those who crudely apply political measuring rods to literature.

And it often happens that both sides in a political struggle—especially, perhaps, when this struggle breaks out in war and violence—will see literature in the same terms. Thus, in an investigation conducted by the British Government after the Easter Rising, a British official claimed, in his testimony, that the Rebellion might have been averted if the Abbey Theatre in Dublin might have had a longer period in which to influence the Irish people. This official saw literature and art in the same terms as did those whom Terence MacSwiney answered in the brief sentence listed above. He merely wanted literature to pour water rather than fire on the spirits of the Irish.

These remarks suggest the relevance of showing permutations in the concept of nationalism and of the nation as we find these in Irish writings. Here, however, there is only space for a few broad illustrations.

The democratic Young Irelanders of 1848 got their ideas from the Great French Revolution. To them, the freedom of Ireland, the creation of a sovereign Irish nation, meant creation of a political condition that would enable Irishmen to realize their dignity and individuality as human beings.

Men like John Mitchel, or the eloquent James Fintan Lalor, who came after Mitchel and the other Young Irelanders, were fighting rebels. They opposed O'Connellism and Daniel O'Connell. John Mitchel and Thomas Davis were cultivated men. They represented a high level of taste and culture in the Ireland of their time. Davis, a ballad singer, critic and essayist, along with his contemporary, the poet James Clarence Mangan, are two of the fathers of modern Irish culture.

Instead of holding to a narrow political conception of culture, men such as Mitchel, Davis, and Mangan had a broader democratic one. Culture was, to them, an instrument which would help the Irish to gain a greater sense of their dignity and individuality as Irishmen.

D. J. O'Donoghue, editor of Davis' essays, wrote concerning Thomas Davis: "In a few words, he sought to impress upon Irishmen the fact that they had much to be proud of in their history and character, and he saw that the surest way to induce a nation to rise to higher things was to imbue them with the idea that they had accomplished much."

John Mitchel in an introduction to Mangan's essays declared that "fresh, manly, vigorous national songs and ballads must by no means be neglected" as one of the ways to be used in rousing the Irish national spirit. It must be stressed that these men were fighting rebels. To them, struggle meant the discovery of the road to manhood.

It is my opinion that the Irish cultural Renaissance is intimately bound up with resurgence of the Irish national spirit, the beginnings of Sinn Fein, the development of the modern Irish labor movement under the leadership of James Connolly and Jim Larkin, and the entire Irish movement in the post-Parnell period.

Following the defeat of Parnell, and the decline of his Irish party until it became a kind of political arena for Eloquent Dempseys, new orientations were developed into so-called Connollyism and Larkinism.

There are no simple causes to be discovered and cited in an attempt to explain the Irish Renaissance. It grew out of a condition in the country. At the same time, it was influenced from without by tendencies from England and the European continent. Fin de siecle esthetics and reflections of French symbolism were brought to Ireland by Yeats and Synge.

The plays of Synge were organized on terms which fit into the esthetic conceptions of men like Pater. Pater also influenced Joyce. George Moore carried into the Renaissance ideas of French naturalism.

Standish O'Grady, usually called the Father of the Renaissance, dealt artistically with the ancient Irish past. He presented the figures of the Irish legends on the Homeric level. A legendary Irish past offered the men of the Renaissance one of their sources of material. They went to the peasantry for speech and language and found among them—especially the peasantry of the west of Ireland—a basis for a language for poetry and for poetic drama. There were pagan elements in the Renaissance. In Yeats' poetry, for instance, definite pagan threads can be observed.

A number of these early figures of the Renaissance were Protestant. They were Anglo-Irish. To this day they and their successors have been criticized on the ground that they were not Irish and did not reflect the Irish spirit. In terms of the strict idea of nationalism which limits Irishmen to Catholics who do not have Anglican antecedents—at least back to the time of Cromwell—this criticism is justified.

But besides being narrow and parochial, it is unhistorical. The Anglo-Irish had all been in Ireland for a long time when the Celtic Renaissance was born. Their influences had become a part of the evolution of Irish history. The movement of these men of the early Renaissance can be interpreted as an effort on their part culturally to enter more fully into the life of Ireland. This is one of the features of the nationalism of the Renaissance.

This national cultural revival, based on the legendary past and on the language of the more economically and socially backward sections of the people, differs from the cultural ideas of the Young Irelanders of 1848. The latter conceived of the Irish as a people.

The characters of the early Irish drama are not a people, but a folk. Formally, the ideas and most of the work produced in the first period of the Renaissance were not political. Politics then didn't enter into this movement in the way that politics entered into the cultural ideas of the Young Irelanders.

If we consider Yeats' poetic drama, *Kathleen ni Houlihan,* we can, perhaps, note this difference more concretely. It is commonly known that when this play was first produced, there were riots, It aroused national resentment.

The lines spoken by simple characters in this poignantly poetic work, and the touching relation of these characters to Kathleen, their symbolic Mother Ireland, brings out the dignity and humanity in Irish peasants. The emphasis in the play is on martyrdom. In effect, Kathleen ni Houlihan calls on her Irish sons to go out and die for Ireland. And, also, we see here that the humanized image of Ireland, created in poetic symbol, is that of an old woman, a sad old woman.

The play most certainly does not fit the cultural prescriptions of Mitchel and Davis. We see this more strongly if we keep in mind the fact that the most popular image of England is John Bull. Along with Kathleen ni Houlihan, the other images created in this period include legendary and pseudo-Homeric figures. Here is a permutation in the Irish national conception as this is mirrored in literature.

At a later date, Padraic Pearse, who was to be executed as a leader of the Easter Rebellion, wrote a play manifestly under the influence of the first period of the Renaissance. The Singer attempts to dramatize the same kind of a mood as does Kathleen ni Houlihan.

The figure of Kathleen is a symbol of a whole nation. The emphasis on martyrdom is generalized by Kathleen. When this emphasis is made in a figure less representative, the generalized mood does not grow out of the play. But the heroic martyrdom of Pearse should be a caution against those inclined to denounce these two plays on purely political grounds.

The creations of this period of the Renaissance—and most notably those of Yeats and Synge—are significant in another way. This work should not be measured by formal conceptions of nationalism, if one seeks a sense of its importance in Irish culture.

Before the Renaissance Irish culture was thin. Genuine work was largely overshadowed by the meretricious. The stage Irishman was often presented as the image of an Irish man.

Synge, Yeats, Lady Gregory and their contemporaries helped bring a note of reality into Irish writing. Their characters have a dignity and a naturalness of their own. Their language bespeaks this dignity. They are real, not false. The reality in all Irish writing which followed them is in their debt. They introduced an image of truth into modern Irish writing.

1974

II
MEMOIRS

Sinclair Lewis

Sinclair Lewis was a tall, thin, nervous man with a pock-marked face. When young, his hair was red, and he was nicknamed "Red." He was the first American writer to receive the Nobel Prize.

During his lifetime, he won as much recognition as, perhaps, any living novelist. His books had big sales all over the world. He added the word "Babbitt" not only to the American language, but also to other languages. He died in Italy in 1951, a lonely man. The accounts of his last days are sad to read. He was far away from the America which, despite his sharp satires, he loved. There seems to have been little sustenance for him in his fame and success. His confidence in himself seemed to have been shattered. The well of lonliness was closing around him; and beyond it was the shadow of approaching death.

My generation in America was profoundly influenced by Lewis. To us, he was a much more influential writer than Ernest Hemingway or William Faulkner. In fact, he was more influential than any American writers of the twentieth century—except perhaps Theodore Dreiser, Sherwood Anderson, and H.L. Mencken.

I first read *Babbitt* when I was 22, a college student. This novel was a great discovery to me; I read it in a state of intense excitement. I laughed; I grew indignant; I saw the traits of George Babbitt in people I knew. There were features of Babbitt in some of my own relatives. By bosses in the big oil corporation for which I worked as a filling-station attendant talked like Babbitt. They lectured at sales meetings as Babbitt might have. Businessmen interviewed in the newspapers often suggested Babbitt.

Lewis's novel revealed aspects of American life with which I had grown up. He wrote of attitudes which I had seen and heard many times, but of which I had not heretofore become conscious. I read, not only in excitement, but also in a growing mood of rebellion. I wanted to protest against the sentimental and forward-looking gospel of service which Babbitt voiced. I did not want the book to end; I wanted to read more. Lewis became one of the writers who helped me liberate myself. He performed this role for many others of my generation. I came to know Sinclair Lewis, but not intimately, in the 1940s. I recall an evening when my wife and I had dinner with him at Luchow's, a restaurant which he, Mencken, and other friends of theirs liked. I was struck by Lewis's loneliness. Several times during the evening, he remarked on how American writers do not see enough of each other and do not talk enough about the problems of writing. He said that they live separate lives and see too little of one another. He also spoke of his native Minnesota and said that it was changing, becoming more cultivated. But he liked New York. In New York, he remarked, he could walk along the streets unrecognized. He avowed that he liked this anonymity. I was not sure that he meant this. He was a celebrity and he had come to care more for the association of celebrities than for relationships with other people. There was some doubt and insecurity in him about his literary position, his talent. He was not as certain of himself as he seemed, or as one would assume. His loneliness was related to some ambivalence in his nature.

One evening he came to my home for dinner. He was quite relaxed, mellowed; and in a mood which was almost sentimental. He spoke warmly, almost lovingly, of Minnesota, of his family, of a brother who had become a doctor. He was genial and seemed to feel quite at ease that evening. But he spoke again of the isolation of American writers.

There was an element of cultural yearning in Sinclair Lewis. His first big success was the novel *Main Street*. The main character, Carol Kennicott, is a culturally frustrated and yearning housewife in a small town in a middle western state like Minnesota. She revolts against the parochialism of her home town. And this all expressed feelings and attitudes of Lewis.

I suspect that there was a definite feeling of rivalry between Sinclair Lewis and Theodore Dreiser. This was exaggerated by charges and countercharges between Dreiser and Lewis's wife, Dorothy Thompson. They accused one another of plagiarism when they both published books concerning a visit to the Soviet Union. At a dinner in honor of the Russian writer

Boris Pilnyak in the early 1930s, Dreiser publicly slapped Lewis in the face. Lewis often paid tribute to Dreiser for the lonely and courageous struggle he had made as a realistic writer. Dreiser pioneered in realistic fiction in America, and met the assaults, attacks and smears of many philistines and of Victorian-minded literary critics, professors and prudes. All writers who came after Dreiser have owed much to him for his struggle. Lewis recognized this, but the two men did not really like each other. Now and then, in a newspaper or magazine, someone would remark that the Nobel Prize had never been awarded to Theodore Dreiser but it had been given to Lewis. From time to time, some critic would declare in public that Dreiser deserved the prize more than Lewis had. I believe this bothered Lewis.

They were different kinds of men. Dreiser was more self-centered and paid less attention to the literary scene and to young writers. One of Lewis's finest traits was his generosity of spirit. He enjoyed discovering new young writers and praising them in public and in literary reviews. He tried to keep up with new books and would constantly recommend the work of young writers. Sometimes, I believe, he was sentimental and overpraised young writers. But it is better to overpraise even out of sentimentality than to neglect and ignore.

I recall a regrettable personal experience with Sinclair Lewis. I sat beside him at a dinner. I was talking in a bantering manner, and I had no thought of him personally in some remarks which I made. I said that the way to become a great writer was to write a bad book. This received excellent reviews and made a lot of money for the author. Then a play, worse than the book but based on it, would make even more money and the writer of the bad book would become more famous. From then on, I said, in parody, a worse musical show, a worse moving picture, a worse radio play and a worse television adaptation would produce a fortune. The worse the work became in the successive adaptations, the more the money rolled in and the greater became the author's fame. Finally, the author died and a biography of him, worse than the book and the successive adaptations, was then written, and once again more money was made as the mills of fame kept on grinding away.

I believed that my parody would amuse Sinclair Lewis. On the contrary, he took personal offense. I never saw him again. He attacked me in print, and after having been pressed by a journalist to say something, I made a retaliatory remark. He told friends that it was proper that I should have done this, and liked my retaliating. He believed that writers should attack one another, a view in contradiction with what he had told me of his feelings about the loneliness and isolation of writers.

On another occasion in the 1940s, I had dinner at his home. We talked of Communism. He dismissed it as a religion. Then we commented on contemporary American literary criticism. I voiced a strong objection to some of the newer American critics and said that they ought to be attacked. He disagreed with me, declaring that a writer must save all of his energy for creative effort. He should not write criticism, engage in controversies or become involved in politics. But, shortly after this, Lewis accepted an assignment reviewing books for a mass-circulation magazine.

All of us are contradictory. I mention the contradictions in Lewis here in order to suggest that he was a man seeking something which he could not find. He saw it as the image of more culture. His books emphasize the gap he observed between a world of culture and sophistication and the provincialism of his native small town of Minnesota. He yearned and sought for the bigger world. And he felt that he had roots in that smaller world which he had satirized out of a feeling of angry love.

Besides *Main Street* and *Babbitt,* his best books are *Arrowsmith, Elmer Gantry* and *Dodsworth.* In America, *Elmer Gantry* has often been underrated and treated as too much of a burlesque. It tells the story of a hypocritical Protestant minister who has a great appetite for life and a talent for fraudulency. Not only is it amusing, but it is also a very true rendering of a type.

Dodsworth presents a businessman in a less satirical light than did *Babbitt.* Because of the fact that he did not rewrite *Babbitt, Dodsworth* was criticized on its appearance. It deals with a trip to Europe by this businessman, and it reveals a searching and seeking quality that was part of Lewis's own character. It is a true characterization, written with feeling. But Lewis had become famous for his satirical characterizations and the critics had stereotyped him. They failed to see the strain of feeling in the man, and they also did not understand that in *Dodsworth* Sinclair Lewis was projecting something of his own problems, his own quest in life.

Lewis did not actively engage in political affairs, but now and then he would take a stand on an issue. He denounced the Moscow Trials of the 1930s as frauds, and in the 1940s, he supported President Roosevelt for reelection. He was a man of liberal spirit and of generous intentions. And he was one of the outstanding American writers of this century. He helped us to see aspects of America more clearly, to create the moods and develop the attitudes which went into the great reforms of the Roosevelt New Deal. At present, his books are not fashionable with the newer generations of

American critics. They look down on writers like Lewis, just as they do on Dreiser and Zola. This will change, and Lewis's place in both American and world literature will be sure and firm.

1955

The Mind of Ben Hecht

"The magic of words," writes Ben Hecht in his autobiography, *A Child of the Century,* "still remains for me. I prefer them to ideas. They are a more precious currency. No ideas have ever filled me with wonder. Phrases have. Ideas become quickly impoverished. Their value, never great, fades with usage. The words are a hardier mintage. Phrases, not ideas, are the tools of re-creating life. Ideas lie on a perpetual rubbish heap, waiting to be salvaged, dusted off, and flaunted anew as riches. The mind, searching pompously for truth, pokes among the fineries of yesterday, rearrays itself in what it has outgrown, parades again its remodelings. The ideas of yesterday, today, and tomorrow are the time, and they add nothing to the meaning of life."

I have given this long quotation not because it gives us insight into the character of ideas and phrases or words but because it tells us much about Hecht. It is difficult for a writer to sustain a 654-page autobiography if he thinks that "ideas lie on a perpetual rubbish heap." He is not equipped to give any clear sense of the meaning of his life and time or of the century of which he is a child. Probably no writer now living (or of the past) could fill 654 pages with phrases that would fill us with the wonder of life if we see phrases in the sense that Ben Hecht does. This is definitely true of Ben Hecht because his best phrases are long since behind him. They can be found in some of his early books—*1001 Afternoons in Chicago,* etc.

Hecht's iconoclasm about and his contempt for ideas does not mean that he is devoid of them. He isn't. But generally his ideas are banal. They repeat what he has said in the yesterday of his own youth. His autobiography is a concoction, an improvised literary cocktail. Everything in life is an occasion for Hecht to sound off, and he fills too many pages with the wind of his prejudices. He tells us what he thinks of ideas and philosophy, of life, love, literature, politics, politicians, Democracy, Communism, Germans and Germany, the Cold War, Jews, Palestine, Zionism, Irgon (the Hebrew Terrorist movement which fought for a Palestinian State), Hollywood, marriages, mistresses, wives, seductions, Chicago, New York, and sundry other matters. All of this could be more interesting if Ben Hecht had more interesting opinions and ideas. But he doesn't and the steam of his phrases, the arrogance of his judgments, and the staleness of many of his prejudices do him a disservice. For Ben Hecht is a gifted writer though he hurts his work because of his easy iconoclasm, his ready-to-wear, medium-priced cynicism, and his deficiency in a clearer sense of values.

At one time, the books of Ben Hecht influenced me. He was the first of the so-called writers of the Chicago Renaissance whom I read. His books stimulated and excited me. Their appeal was varied. A phrase of his, "the greedy little half-dead," caught my eye. I repeated it often in youthful discussions of life and humanity. I stood on street corners in the Loop, staring at the faces in the passing crowd, seeking closer contact with people, trying to feel more and understand them better, and at the same time, I told myself that they were "the greedy little half-dead." This gave me a feeling of importance. I had a phrase which helped me feel superior to the great mass of humanity. I had words which could lift me above the lusts, the confusions, the ignorance, the cruelties, the sadnesses, and the vain strivings of many people.

I was a student at the University of Chicago and I worked in a filling station behind the Stockyards at Thirty-fifth and Morgan. There, more of "the greedy little half-dead" would pass. I would stand inside the service station, gazing at the mob and trying to describe them in phrases like those of Ben Hecht. This was both frustrating and stimulating. I had read *1001 Afternoons in Chicago* along with *Count Bruga*. It ranks in my opinion as Hecht's best book. It consists of sketches Hecht wrote for the *Chicago Daily News* and is full of charm, color, and exciting phrases. Hecht's best talent is that of coining metaphors, and he was at his peak when he knocked off *1001 Afternoons in Chicago*. His subjects are usually grotesque. The grotesque has usually interested him and to it, he brings a sense of the mordant. In *A Child of the Century,* he boasts of his interest in the sordid—in hangings, rapes, and murders.

"I could fill over a hundred pages with lists of fascinating cadavers."

1001 Afternoons in Chicago helped me to become more aware of, let us say, the poetry of the street. Its high-voltage figures of speech attracted me. Frequently, the young and aspiring writer sees the use of figures of speech, the coining of phrases, as the sign of literary talent. I did. Ben Hecht could make phrases. Harry Hansen, in *Mid-West Portraits,* characterized him as a Pagliacci of the fire escapes. *1001 Afternoons in Chicago* consists of sketches. They are short and Hecht's talents were fresh; he had an exhuberance and flair. His novels *Erik Dorn* and *Humpty Dumpty* were frustrating. They exuded a sense of the present, of life going on immediately in one's own time, and there was some excitement in this. (What little sense of books and culture I had had come to me, almost as though by osmosis, from the dead Victorian past.) There was a frankness about sex but the cynicism, the iconoclasm, the verbal posturings, the lack of empathy frustrated me. A newspaper man can look at people and happenings; he can cast a cold and jaundiced eye at politicians; he can watch hangings; he can dig into tales of rape and murder; and he can do a good piece of reporting without having to identify deeply with the people who are subjects of his stories. A fair number of journalists tend to develop what sometimes seems to be an occupational trait—they tend to regard what happens as though it occurred so that they could do a story. The world is a show made for them. Hecht often gives the impression that this is an integral feature of the way he looks at life. Journalism is an honorable and socially useful profession. I do not intend to denegate it. But what I have observed might help explain why it is often so difficult for journalists to write novels. This may be the case in Hecht's novels. *Count Bruga* was an exception but it is a special kind of book. The chief protagonist is a poet who acts and talks much like a once well-known Chicago poet. The character is bizarre and Hecht has a lively and enthusiastic feeling for the bizarre.

Behind the frustration I found in Hecht's early novels, there was not only a limited power to identify; there was too little sympathy. Sympathy is usually significant because it is the means of making human emotions important. I discovered Sherwood Anderson and Theodore Dreiser after Hecht. In them, I found not cleverness or a keenness for a grotesque surface of life or an iconoclasm that helped me feel a false sense of superiority to others; but rather, in them, I encountered a seriousness of feeling about human emotions, human tragedies, about the struggle, often so blundering, which we all make to live out our life span. There are some writers who can produce out of negative emotions, who can arouse and move us. Celine, in *Journey to the End of Night* and *Death on the Installment Plan,* is one. But Celine hates and hates deeply. His hatred, in fact, is so intense that it carries its own antidote. As we read, we can purge ourselves of hatred. Ben Hecht doesn't hate; he flings out phrases of contempt. He laughs. He falls into quick scorn; is facilely negative. He is something of a Chicago Hupmann without any real cultivation or depth of feeling.

A *Child of the Century* echoes Ben Hecht's other writings, including his plays and movie scenarios. There are remembrances of *1001 Afternoons in Chicago, The Front Page, Erik Dorn, A Jew in Love,* and of many motion pictures jumbled up with readily given offhand judgments on almost all of the complicated world of today. By being so confidently judgmental, Ben Hecht does damage to his book; he reduces the effect that he might have achieved. Frequently, he asserts a dislike for people. "The greedy little half-dead" of the twenties are redescribed as "the half-alive ones." "They are not individuals and the modern world is witnessing the decline and death of individuality." "The twentieth century died at the end of the 1920s. Free speech is a mirage." "The deepest American fear has not been fear of censorship as much as fear of being censorable." And, "My countrymen think actually in the same manner as do the conforming Russians." And, "We have an embryonic police state in America." And, "There are the laurelled notables who, though they seem to be writing eruditely and aloofly, are doing nothing more than exhausting their minds in holding together the biases and errors in which they live. Such to my mind was Santayana." And, "Individual man is being remade as a faceless part of Democracy, Socialism, Communism and Fascism. Although at variance in mood and practice, all modern political systems make for the same goal posts—here to run world most conveniently for the crowd." And, many people are "too weak to resist the tidal wave of education."

Had a few more splashes from that wave hit Ben Hecht, it might not have damaged him. And as for individuality, there is little of it in what I have quoted and paraphrased from his many absolutistic generalizations.

You keep wading through this kind of individuality from the mind and pen of a militant individualist and you recall your own adolescent self-assertiveness. You remember that you once knew less than Ben Hecht knows, talked as big, and shocked people. All this did was give you a cheap pseudo sense of pleasure. Suddenly, you come out of this pop-gun fire of words and read a good anecdote. You see that the author is a man who can be perceptive. You are held by well-done vignettes which are as effective as were the sketches of *1001 Afternoons in Chicago*.

Ben Hecht writes with warmth and love of his family, his parents, aunts and uncles. He describes touchingly a scene when he went to dine with his parents and to tell them that he had left his first wife and was living with another woman. Here, convention was flouted, and his parents were conventional people. But how differently he handles the flouting of convention in recounting this scene from the way he does when he flings out worn-down banalities of the twenties. He becomes a man of perception; he senses his parents' feelings.

Reading this scene, we know that the author is a man of talent and perception, as well as one who speaks of serious problems with shallow cynicism.

Most interesting in his autobiography are the descriptions of childhood scenes in Racine, Wisconsin, and of his early newspaper days in Chicago. He pens little portraits of newspaper men and editorial offices, of himself as a working journalist of the *Front Page* variety and of figures involved in the Chicago Literary Renaissance. He has unpleasant anecdotes to tell of Sherwood Anderson. His description of Maxwell Bodenheim is accurate but on the sentimental side. Different is his account of how Carl Sandburg became a journalist, and his warm characterization of the late Henry Justin Smith. The latter is revealed as an unusual managing editor. And there is also a sympathetic portrait of Stanislas Szukalski, the strange and seemingly mad Polish sculptor who lived in Chicago for years. If one can stand Hecht's empty pontificating, or learn to skip it, *A Child of the Century* offers some rewarding and interesting reading.

Hecht has much to say of New York and of Hollywood in the twenties. He tells anecdotes, gossips about the drawn characterizations of Hollywood, Broadway, and New York literateurs. But Hecht loved Chicago. His accounts of his experiences and of his friends there are worth more than what he has to report on New York and Hollywood. Trappings of glamour shroud his comments of New York and Hollywood; sentimentality sometimes oozes out of the hard-boiled reporter.

He also describes two years of reporting in Germany immediately after the end of the First World War. But the equipment of the young journalit and writer of *1001 Afternoons in Chicago* did not serve him will in understanding a society and nation torn by war and in the throes of a revolutionary situation. He gives a distorted and even flippant account of German events of 1919 and 1920. And there is crass vulgarity in an anecdote about Karl Liebknecht, the martyred German Socialist who voted alone in the German Reichstag of 1914 against the war and who was murdered by reactionary German rightists. He has much to say of his experiences as a co-chairman of committees supporting Irgon, the Palestinian terrorist movement, and is contemptuous of Jews who did not follow him in support of this movement. He was of considerable help to Irgon, but there is something romantic and quixotic about this venture into revolutionary politics. There are blanket condemnations of a host of Jews and Gentiles from the late President Roosevelt down because they did not act in consonnance with the Irgon programme. In effect, he tells anecdotes which would almost put the stamp of anti-Semitism on the late President Roosevelt. I cannot comment on the Palestinian situation because I am not sufficiently well informed. But, just as extreme Irish nationalists and die-hards have convinced me that they are romantically rigid, so does Ben Hecht make me suspicious of the soundness of his judgment on the complicated Palestinian history of recent years.

He tells us of his swimming pool on his Nyack, New York estate, of the big money he made in Hollywood, of some of the parties he gave. There are sprinkling comments on the love-life among the stars and in the bordello.

One man he deeply admired was H. L. Mencken. He shares many of Mencken's attitudes. While having the energy, there is none of the Mencken gusto in Hecht's assaults on booberty. Also, unlike Mencken, Hecht gives no evidence of having read as much as Mencken. Thus, Mencken's views are grounded on a more serious foundation than Hecht's.

Seen now and in the past, Ben Hecht appears a man of talent, of easy prejudices, and without values. Unlike in the twenties, he cannot today stimulate youth. He has seen and reported the grotesque and sordid but it now appears on his pages as something too familiar.

He writes: "Except for my relation to God, I have not changed in forty years. I have not become different as an adult."

It seems a shame that a man of talent who has had the opportunities in life that Ben Hecht has had would be pleased to keep sitting on what he styles as his "Pedestal of Sameness."

This comes as a strange boast from a man who defends—even rants against—the destruction of individuality in our country. Iconoclasm can be as conventional as conventionality. And this child of the century appears to be a conventional iconoclast. The "half-alive ones," the mob, the people drowned by the "tidal wave of education"—they have not changed. But here is one of the not-half-alive, here is one of the alive ones; and he does not give us a great outpouring of his aliveness.

Talent could be better used.

1955

Nathaniel West

An American writer of the 1930s beginning to receive attention is Nathaniel West. His complete works have been published by Farrar, Strauss and Cudahy. This book includes *The Dream Life of Balso Snell, Miss Lonelyhearts, A Cool Million,* and *The Day of the Locust.*

I'm glad that "Pop" West is finally receiving his literary due. Pop was an excellent writer, a man with literary talent. He was more of a writer than I realized when I first met him in the early thirties. He was a big man, serious, and somewhat restrained. He spoke reflectively about books; his judgments were based both on his love of literature and his own particular problems as a writer. His thoughts and remarks were always honest and clear. But when I knew him, he was forming and clarifying his opinions and literary views. I saw him only once after 1935 and then it was an accidental meeting on the street. I do not know how his literary thinking have evolved or changed in the last years of his life.

But back in the early thirties when I saw him from time to time, he was interested in so-called realistic writing. He disagreed with the claims and contentions put forth for proletarian writing. He believed that writers should be free; that they shouldn't take instruction or dictation from political people or movements.

He was a kind man and a friendly one. For a while he managed a hotel here in New York. When my wife and I were evicted from our apartment (a not too uncommon experience during the Depression), Pop let us stay in a suite of rooms for two weeks. He had no intemperate habits, and once he reproved me, but not in a hostile way but in the manner of a friend.

Nathaniel West had great skill, more skill and talent than warmth. His writing is grotesque in its ironies, parodies, and caricatures. His bite was deep, too deep to permit laughter. In fact, I don't recall Pop laughing very much. He was serious about literature and continued to develop as a writer. He died young but it can be assumed that had his career not been cut short, he would have become a truly distinguished writer. His last book, *The Day of the Locust*, is considered his best book by many. It is about Hollywood and can be read as a savage indictment. He used to talk about this book, about odd and grotesque characters he had met in Hollywood. Toward the end of the book, there is a strong touch of this very Hollywood that West was indicting. Still, it is one of the important novels of the thirties.

Miss Lonelyhearts is the story of a reporter who conducts a column of advice to the lovelorn. It reveals West's capacity to depict the grotesque. In his preparation for this work, Nathaniel West read William James' *The Varieties of Religious Experience*. Through satire, caricature, and a comedia presentation which reveals too much horror to be truly comic, Nathaniel West was working towards his own sense of people, of humanity.

His early death cut him down in mid-path. We cannot be sure what might have been but we can be sure that the books he left behind deserve attention.

Nathaniel West was both an interesting and a talented writer.

1958

A Chance Meeting with
Mencken and Masters

One fine night, early in August 1935, actress Hortense Alden and I were
taking a walk. Passing the Hotel Brevoort, she looked at the people seated
at the sidewalk cafe and suddenly exclaimed:
"Oh, there's H.L. Mencken."
I had corresponded with Mencken and he had published writings of
mine during his last days as an editor of *The American Mercury*. We went
over to him and I introduced myself. He was glad to see me; he already
knew Hortense Alden. He asked us to sit down and introduced us to the
somewhat seedy looking gentleman at his table. It was Edgar Lee Masters.
Once these men had been big events in my life. When I read *Spoon
River Anthology* in 1927 it had carried me away. I thought that it was a
great book, and to this day, I have not changed my mind about it. And besides the fact that I was one of the last younger writers whom Mencken
liked and published, I had, in the twenties, read him with great eagerness.
He had been a healthy influence upon me.
We had a beer and talked. Mencken was most cordial, and almost
from the first moment that I had met him, I could readily perceive that
here was a true gentleman. My first impression of him physically was that
he looked perhaps like a butcher boy. Masters was a big man but he had already begun to age. He laughed like an old man and he seemed to exude a
sense of deep melancholy. We had not talked long before I clearly realized
how there was a difference of generations separating me from them. Much
as I respected them, pleased as I was to meet them, I quickly felt that time

and events had passed them by. I had not yet lost a conceit of my own generation, which is fairly common and which so frequently distorts the feelings and impressions of young writers.

At the time, there was excitement over the Italian-Ethiopian situation and dread that it might lead to the Second World War. Hortense Alden asked Mencken what he thought of the prospective Italian invasion of Ethiopia. He answered that he had not thought much about it one way or the other, and that he did not see how it could be of much importance. I remarked that it appeared to me as though the Pope would support such an invasion. This provoked both Mencken and Masters to joke and they said, in raillery, that of course if the Pope supported an invasion, they would have to be for it. They told each other that after all, they were both Christians. This was one of their private, personal jokes. Mencken then reminded Masters that the latter was a Methodist. I joined in the talk, reminding them both that, after all, they were both Protestants. I hesitated to say what my old Irish grandmother might have said about that fact. We laughed.

Earlier that year, there had been a strike of the office workers at *The American Mercury*. Mencken mentioned the strike, and said that the girls would have gotten everything they asked for, but that they had been tricked by a dirty bunch of Communists. I didn't agree with him then, but now, looking back, it is my belief that this strike was Communist-led, and I think that he probably was right in his judgment.

He went on to tell me that I shouldn't allow myself to get mixed up in such matters. An artist, he added, had no place in politics.

Masters declared that he knew nothing about Communism, except that it was a brand of Boganism. They both found much amusement in William Jennings Bryan, and for him, they had jolly contempt.

Then Mencken said that after both he and Masters died in another hundred years, one poet who would be remembered was Kipling, the Kipling of *Barrack Room Ballads*. Remembering how I had read Kipling with such pleasure back in my college days and earlier, I avowed a liking for his *Barrack Room Ballads*. Mencken then said that Kipling was crazy and had been since his son had been killed in the war. Also, he told us that when people invited Kipling out in England, they took great precautions because he was liable to stand on a table and goddamn them all.

Masters then said that he was bringing out a book of poems, and also a book on the late Vachel Lindsay. Masters had deep respect for Lindsay and believed that Lindsay had never received his due as

a poet. Invariably, he talked of Lindsay on later occasions when I saw him.
Masters said that Lindsay killed himself drinking Lysol and was crazy.
Mencken said that Lindsay was the craziest poet in America and a freak.

Then Mencken spoke about George Sterling, the dead poet. Right
after Sterling's death, he received a letter from a girl, an old sweetheart of
Sterling's. She sent him some poems written to her by Sterling. A few
days later, still another girl wrote him and sent him the same poems. Sterling had made his poems do more than double duty with his girl friends.
This he said was confidential. Leaning toward me, he added:

"Farrell, keep that under your ear."

He went on talking, with relish and enjoyment. Mencken liked to
talk and, as I was to learn later, he was a good conversationalist.

He said that the greatest of all newspaper men was a fellow named
George Stevens, but instead of elaborating on this remark, he switched to
literature and said that perhaps the greatest short story ever written was
Joseph Conrad's "Youth." Also he spoke warmly and in praise of the writer Josephine Herbst.

Then he spoke of the Communists. He said that he had nothing a-
gainst the Communists. They were like Christian Scientists and New Dealers, except that they had a more coherent viewpoint than New Dealers.
New Dealers were merely mulcting the people. And Huey Long. At that
time, Long was constantly in the news, and only a few months previously,
he had conducted his filibuster in the Senate. I had seen it and told Mencken about it.

Mencken predicted flatly that within six months, Huey Long would
be assassinated in Louisiana.

And Father Coughlin, who was then in the news and was regarded by
many as a dangerous fascist? Mencken said that Father Coughlin was polit-
ically dead.

Warming up, he spoke of the Scopes trial and enthusiastically said
that it was the greatest show ever held in America, and the greatest newspaper feature. Then he told of a joke he had played on a minister whom
we will here call Reverend Mellon. Meeting the Reverend Mellon during the
trial, Mencken told him that the Reds were coming down from Cincinnati
to destroy civilization. Alarmed, the Reverend Mellon went into action,
telegraphing the Governor of the state. Cops were sent into the town and
people coming by train from Cincinnati were arrested. Then about three
o'clock of the same afternoon, Mencken and the Reverend Mellon again

met, and the minister told Mencken about the Red invasion from Sodom, Cincinnati, and of the precautions taken to repel it.

When we spoke of poetry, Masters said that he had not read Robinson Jeffers or most new stuff. He had, however, read the poetry of Archibald MacLeish. He didn't say whether he liked or disliked it.

Mencken then praised some of the short stories of Richard Harding Davis. Changing the subject, he remarked that he had hired Charlie Augoff to work on *The American Mercury* on the basis of a guess. It had worked out well and he spoke warmly of Augoff, Masters, cutting in, spoke of an American poet, remarking that this poet had hated everybody in a dress suit until he, himself, had gotten one.

But there were a few moments different in character, and Mencken revealed another side of himself, mainly by silence, understatement and a change of expression. His wife had died recently. This had cut him up, deeply saddened him.

A newspaper man whom I had known in Paris, Wambly Bald, came over and spoke with us for a few moments. He recalled having interviewed Mencken once. Talk ran on in the same vein. There were more jokes about Bryan and the Methodists. Then they left, but on leaving, Mencken formally bowed to Hortense Alden.

My inner judgment was cruel. I liked them but as I watched them leave, I thought that they were becoming fossilized. Again, a conceit of my own time and generation came into my thinking. I saw both men again and my view of them changed. My conceit dropped away from me with a few more years of experience. I watched them walk away, up Fifth Avenue, and also watched the big double deck green buses passing them. Life, the times, a changing world was passing them by like buses rolling along Fifth Avenue.

I enjoyed the evening. In fact I was flattered to have met them both. And they had met me with ease and naturalness, speaking as they would if alone. They were warm friends and Mencken almost always spent an evening with Masters when he came to New York. They had their jokes, their humor, their fun railing at death, remembering writers who were widely ignored by a newer generation, joshing and laughing about the wowsers, the Methodists and other actors in what they regarded as the great American show.

Masters' reputation was already on the wane, and these nights with Mencken and Mencken's friendship were of great and perhaps singular importance to him.

Masters was melancholy, and at times bitter. With Mencken he lightened up, and spoke dryly. He laughed more on that night when I first met them than he did on other occasions when I saw him.

Mencken was extrovert, and very friendly without being intimate. He was jolly and liked to tell anecdotes and stories.

I saw them disappear on Fifth Avenue. I thought there were two of the legends of my own life, two legends of American literature.

1965

William McFee, 1881–1966

It was over forty years ago that I picked up a novel—it had a red cover—and started reading it. The name of the book was *Casuals of the Sea*. The author's name, William McFee.

The year was 1925, a time when the appeal of the sea was romantic for a young man. Many of us dreamed of adventures in far-flung ports. We had grown up on stories of the Wild West which was no longer wild. Jack London, Joseph Conrad, Rudyard Kipling pointed to another road of adventure—the open sea.

William McFee was a ship's engineer; and he was an artist. He was aware of the motors and the machinery; he heard both the noise and the music of them. He knew the appeal of the sea. And yet William McFee was different because of the difference in the order of his perception. He could hear the roar of an ocean swell; and he could hear the motors turn. He could smell the briny air and he could smell the fumes of the acetylene torch. This gave him a range of perceptions and a body of knowledge which was his own—by education and by profession.

And the artist in him was concerned with the fiats of human destiny.

II

When William McFee wrote, he was still an engineer. But he was more. He was a literary artist. He enriched and enlarged the resources, the subject matter, and the contents of the English language.

Today, he has been passed by in the trivialities of fashion. But it is no more than a momentary eclipse in the continuity of life. Because William McFee was an artist in the truest sense of the word; and his books will remain with us. They must. There can be no surrender by artists to fad and fashion. There must be solidarity to preserve the continuity of mankind.

III

William McFee was born in the year 1881. He died in 1966 at the age of eighty-five. His was a long life. And now, he has gone to a long sleep. William McFee is no more. But there are many of us whom his books helped to awaken; and there will be more. Through his books, Willaim McFee will continue to live.

Hail and Farewell, William McFee—your name has been implanted in the memory of mankind.

1966

A Paris Memoir

It almost happened that my first book was not *Young Lonigan,* the first volume of my "Lonigan" trilogy. In 1931, Ezra Pound attempted to get four of my stories published in England as a book. I had sent many stories from Chicago to Samuel Putnam, author of *Paris Was Our Mistress.* Sam was originally from Chicago. He was living in Paris. In 1929, he was an editor of the quarterly *This Quarter,* and he slipped into an issue a short story, "Studs," which was one of the sources of the genesis of "Studs Lonigan." *This Quarter* was edited by E. Titus, who was the original publisher of *Lady Chatterley's Lover.*

Sam Putnam and Titus had a falling out. He and Peter Neagre, a Roumanian who became a naturalized American, and who wrote stories in English, made plans to launch a quarterly, *The New Review.* Sam Putnam invited Ezra Pound, then living at Rapallo, to come in with them.

Pound liked my stories and wrote Sam about them enthusiastically. He compared one, "The Scarecrow," with the writings of Henry James.

I went to Paris, arriving there in April, 1931. Ezra came to Paris in May, and I had lunch with him in a restaurant on the rue Carmartain.

Ezra was very friendly, and spoke most enthusiastically of my writing. He selected four of my early stories, "The Scarecrow," "Looking 'Em Over," "Meet the Girls," and "Honey We'll Be Brave," and said that he would like to see them published. He tried to get an English publisher for them. An English writer, still living and of some reputation, read these stories and his reaction was violently angry and melodramatically contemptuous.

Ezra arranged for me to go to see Desmond Harmsworth, who had a rented Paris apartment on the Isle Saint Louis. Desmond Harmsworth lived in the same building as did Ramon Fernandez of the *Nouvelle Revue Française.*

Desmond Harmsworth was the son of Lord Harmsworth, who was one of the owners of the Lord Norincliffe press holdings. He, Desmond Harmsworth (later Lord Harmsworth), was a pleasant, polite, civilized and noncommittal young Englishman. He was most cordial to me. He did not, however, accept my stories for the publishing firm that he had but recently launched. He took them, they were read, and Desmond Harmsworth, spoke well of them. But he did not believe that he could publish them.

Later, however, I did succeed in getting him to publish a book of a friend of mine. This friend was a Danish sculptor, Adam Fischer. He was living in Montrouge, a *banlieu* of Paris.

Adam Fischer was a solid and sensitive sculptor, and he had known many of the French post-Impressionistic painters. He had known Diego Rivera, too. In his home, I saw many of Rivera's early paintings, hanging on the walls. I also met Diego's first wife there, one evening.

Adam Fischer, an imaginative man, had taken a series of pictures which depicted the fantasy journey of his twelve-year-old daughter's dolls when the dolls "got mad" at her for leaving them to go to Paris. It was a family venture, and a poetic sense of reality and fantasy was captured, with a use of safety pins, and screws, sticks, many common things, to arrange scenic backgrounds for the pictures. I was much taken by these pictures. They were arranged in a loose serial order, and the pictures told a lovely, imaginative story. It was called "The Dolls' Journey."

I phoned Desmond Harmsworth, and made an appointment to bring Adam Fischer with the pictures of "The Dolls' Journey." He was taken with the pictures. He practically accepted the book on sight. It was published. However, it never attracted much attention.

It was and is a lovely book.

I have not been in touch with Desmond Harmsworth (I believe that he is still living) for more than twenty-five years. But I have always remembered him with pleasing thoughts, because of his response to Adam Fischer's book.

This is a reminiscence which I believe will interest some readers today. Hence, I have written it, here.

1967

A Remembrance of
Ernest Hemingway

I met Ernest Hemingway in Key West, in 1936. To me, he was very genial, friendly, and hospitable. I had been in Key West for a few days before I sent him a note. Upon receiving it at his post box, he came to the rooming house where I was staying, immediately.

I had known his family in Oak Park. Ernest expressed disappointment that I had not immediately looked him up in Key West.

One of the first things he said to me was that when he had read the fight scene in *Young Lonigan* he had known that the writer had it, and knew what he was writing about.

One of my first remarks to Ernest was to josh him.

"Hemingway," I said, "I am going to write a book, titled 'Death at 3 P.M. on the Diamond.' Chapter One will be 'The Heroism of Ty Cobb's Hook Slide.' Chapter Two will be 'The Pathos of Lefty Grove's Outcurve.' Chapter Three will be 'The Tragic Stance of Paul Waner in the Batter's Box.' Chapter Four will be 'The Sadness in the Eyes of Silk McLaughlin When He Calls a Man Out at Home Plate.' "

Ernest burst out in hearty laughter. My playful parodying of "Death in the Afternoon" amused him.

We talked about prize fighting. Ernest explained why Gene Tunney defeated Jack Dempsey for the heavyweight championship of the world.

"Dempsey was a hooker. Tunney was a straight puncher."

I quoted this remark to Gene Tunney.

"Yes, that's true," Gene said.

Ernest believed that Gene Tunney was one of the greatest of heavyweight champions. I think I would concur.

Ernest and Gene Tunney were loyal friends. Gene Tunney is loyal to Ernest's memory. He tells interesting anecdotes about his friendship with Ernest.

I also talked with Ernest about *jai alai,* or *pelota,* or *fronton.* I was pleased to learn that he was enthusiastic about this sport. He knew some of the players.

"Piston and Guillermo are probably the greatest *jai alai* players in the world," I said.

Ernest knew them. He shared my admiration for them both.

Piston played up front, and Guillermo played back. Sometimes they would be matched against three players.

Piston was flashy and graceful. He could catch hard rebounds with his *cesta,* while playing up pretty close to the front wall. He was skillful in placing shots, and frequently he would catch his opposition off balance. One return he had perfected was a two-wall carom shot that was virtually non-returnable. He would catch a rebound, close up, on his right and close to the side lines. When he used this carom shot, he let the *pelota* go out of his *cesta* quick but with speed and neat precision. The *pelota* was directed at an acute angle near to the juncture of the front and side wall. It bounded off the front wall, to the left, hit the left wall a couple of yards or less from the juncture of the two walls. Then, the *pelota* rebounded off the side line, fast, and at an acute angle. It came back fast and more or less to where Piston had started the shot. And it hit inside of sidelines by a foot, or even inches. It was a mean, effective shot.

Guillermo was a big man, but fast on his feet. It was a task to get the *pelota* by him so that he would fail to make a return. He ran up the walls, and made returns. He showed what is called "class."

Ernest agreed, too, that Guillermo was probably the world's greatest *pelota* player.

1968

The Eternal Question of
John O'Hara

Sometimes, when a man dies, upon hearing the news of his death, we have an instant comprehension of what the man was, what he meant or did not mean, and what the significance of his life work was.

This is often my experience when I hear of the passing of a writer.

The death of John O'Hara was front page news in *The New York Times*. However, the long obituary did not say very much.

And this was my feeling about John O'Hara as a writer when I was told of his death.

John O'Hara's real gift was as a short story writer. He was good, very good, at this. Had he concentrated his best energies on the output of short stories, he might have become a very distinguished (but lesser) Guy de Maupassant in American literature.

Guy de Maupassant was a great writer but he was a derivative writer. John O'Hara was a good writer and he too was a derivative writer. By derivative, I do not mean a writer who merely imitates. His derivation is revealed in his insights, his range, his way of seeing life. He absorbs a cultural, literary, and social atmosphere easily. But what he has actually absorbed is the already interpreted, the already expressed, and the already evaluated.

It is evident that a derivative writer is more likely to excel in short stories than in novels. He is more likely to give a sharper and more impressive emphasis to his relatively limited originality. This was the story of John O'Hara.

But one of John O'Hara's novels was outstanding. This was *Appointment in Samarra*. In this novel, O'Hara attained what Henry James called "saturation." I interpret this word to mean that the characters and their environment, including their cultural, social, and moral background, become a world, or a segment of a world, with a past and a present, and an assumable future, and with a play of meanings.

Another of John O'Hara's achievements was *Pal Joey*. He wrote the book from which the musical was adapted. It was delightful. It was notably free of cheapness, something very unusual in a Broadway musical that becomes a hit. But it was only delightful.

John O'Hara became an American literary name with the publication of *Butterfield 8*, originally published in 1934. The book was written with a hard, firm objectivity. It was of a subject matter that lends itself to sentimentality. There is no sentimentality in *Butterfield 8*. Its absence, the sure and often crisp objectivity, is almost the opposite of sentimentality. *Butterfield 8* was well written. It had the character of immediacy in a playtime world symbolized by the special nightclub, 21. It was *au courant* with the part-time lives of people who spend and play and drink and talk— all with an uncertain sense of the reality of what they are doing. But then, it was no more than *au courant*.

The title of another of John O'Hara's novels, *A Rage to Live*, presents the same shallow current. There is no rage at all in *A Rage to Live*, only a tantrum. It is a directionless work of an unconventional escape from what an eighteenth century Frenchman called "the dread of unimporance."

John O'Hara's novel *The Big Laugh* contains, on the first page, the following:

By the time a man is forty his people—his family, friends, acquaintances, enemies, and even total strangers who have some reason to be aware of his existence—have decided what kind of man he is. Their judgment may be wrong, but it is their judgment and it is usually final because people in a group lack the patience to reconsider the evidence they have on one man .... It is therefore unreasonable for any man to expect or to hope for a second mass human judgment that will improve his standing. By the same token, although a man may fall from grace, he will continue to enjoy the good will of those who had earlier convinced themselves that he was a good man. People who have made up their minds about a man do not like to have their opinions changed, to reverse their judgments on account of some new evidence or new arguments, and the man who tries to compel them to change their minds is at least wasting his time, and he may be asking for trouble.

This is easy generalization, a known kind of wisdom, partly true and of no particular illumination. One is tempted to ask, "So what?" This may seem an ungenerous way to talk of a writer just dead, but the point is this: John O'Hara was a professional, and he was good enough to be talked about without false sentiment. He knew how to write dialogue, how to write a crisp prose and how to tell a story. But now that he is dead, you have to ask about the significance of his life work. John O'Hara wrote distinguished short stories and could not write distinguished novels? I find myself wondering why he never became, with all his natural talent, a great writer. This will be the eternal question about his work.

1970

Memories of New York

I first came to New York in July of 1927. I had hitchhiked from Chicago
with a friend, Paul Caron. We arrived with a few dollars in our pockets,
and slept on a bench in Union Square on our first night. Driving into the
city, through the Bronx, with a family that had picked us up, I had thought
of Balzac's character, Rastignac in *Pere Goriot*. In my mind, I shook my
fists at the city as he had, and said to myself: "Henceforth, there will be
war between us."

I was determined to become a writer. And New York was a powerful magnet, attracting the ambitious youth of the country. During those
first days in New York, I would – many times – tell myself:

"I'm here. I'm in New York."

Paul and I lived on less than a dollar a day. Our room rent at the
Mills Hotel on West 36th Street at the corner of Seventh Avenue was thirty-
five cents a night. The hotel still stands there but the name is changed and
the cost per night has gone up. We ate, mostly in Automat cafeterias, on
fifty cents a day. For breakfast, we had muffins and coffee for ten cents.
For lunch and for dinner, we had beans and coffee for twenty cents. In
between we went hungry – unless we were flush – and then we might have
extra coffee and muffins.

We managed to get jobs fairly quickly. We were both young and we
could talk fast and big when we applied for work. My first job was as a
clerk for the United Cigar Company at a store at 96th Street and Broadway.
From there, I was transferred to a store at 72nd and Broadway. My salary

began at $24 a week. After a few weeks, it rose to $26 and then to $28. But I found a better job selling space in the R.R. Donnelly Red Book in Queens at $35 a week. In those days, that was a good salary.

For a while I lived in a rooming house for $7 a week. It was over a drug store at 8th Street and Fifth Avenue. But the rent included bedbugs so I moved to the YMCA at 23rd Street of Seventh Avenue. The rent there also was $7 a week. I was one of the most affluent of the guests. Many of the others envied me my "position"—not only because of the salary but because I did not work regular hours. I went out to my territory in Queens when I felt like it. I was able to sell enough in a few hours a week to keep my job. I spent more time in libraries than I did selling.

I hungered for people, for girls, for intelligent males. I hungered for the literary atmosphere but knew no one in that world. I used to wander around Greenwich Village. I would go to Hubert's cafeteria which was on Sheridan Square. It was always crowded with young people – Bohemians, long-haired fellows and short-haired girls. There were always some young fellows who had the mark of conventionality on them, young men from the Bronx and Queens who were out slumming. I was too shy to talk to any of the Bohemians I saw; all I did was watch.

There was much contrast – wealth and poverty; grandeur and misery. Every night, homeless, lonely men lined up to get their thirty-five cent cubicles at the Mills Hotel. A few older men were shabbily well-dressed, others looked like bums. A few blocks away was Broadway with its bright lights, marquees, advertising signs, crowded streets and its generally gaudy atmosphere.

I saw and recognized Maxwell Bodenheim looking seedy and sardonic on the steps of the New York Public Library at 42nd Street and Fifth Avenue. He was holding, prominently displayed under his arm, a copy of his novel, *Replenishing Jessica.* I spent hours in the General Reading Room. There were free lectures and concerts. There was the Metropolitan Museum of Art. New York was not only a city of adventure; but it was also a university. I could read books, free. Concerts were free. For just a few dollars, I could attend theaters. I saw the Abbey Players with Sara Allgood do *The Plough and the Stars.* I saw Walter Hampton in an Ibsen revival. And I saw a production of Paul Green's *In Abraham's Bosom* at the Provincetown Players in the Village.

It was lonely and frustrating but I was full of eagerness, as well as loneliness, for the future and for success. I was fighting my Balzacian war with the city to more or less of a draw.

[94]

Since then, I have lived in New York for over forty years. It remains a fascinating city.

1974

III
REVIEWS

The Collected Stories of
Isaac Babel

"Are words necessary? A man was," writes Isaac Babel in his short story "How It Was Done in Odessa," "and is no more. A harmless bachelor was living his life like a bird on a bough, and had to meet a nonsensical end. There came a Jew looking like a sailor and took a potshot not at some clay pipe or dolly but at a live man. Are words necessary?"

This paragraph not only suggests something of the attitude and irony of Babel as a writer but it also takes on significance when we realize that this great writer became one of the disappeared in the Soviet Union. Babel was born in Odessa in 1894 of middle-class Jewish parents. During the Revolution and Civil War he occupied minor posts. He fought with Budenny's cavalry during the Polish campaign. His writing was admired by Gorky and hailed by Leon Trotsky, who was more perceptive of literature than any of the other early Bolshevik leaders.

At a Writers Congress held in the Soviet Union in 1934, Babel delivered a speech in which he ironically joked about himself as practicing a new literary genre. He said that he was "the master of the genre of silence." For a number of years, Babel, who as an artist approached the stature of Chekhov, was silent. Since 1936, his name has not been mentioned in Soviet literary publications. He was arrested and incarcerated in a concentration camp in 1937. The reason for this is not known. Then, in 1939 or 1940, he "died" in the camp.

Thinking of this great writer, one can well paraphrase from his own work: "Are words necessary?"

A great artist, either directly or indirectly, was destroyed by a totalitarian police state.

In *The Collected Stories* are included Babel's famous stories from *Cavalry*. These dealt with life in Budenny's army. They were originally translated and published in America by Alfred Knopf in 1929. It was on the basis of this that Babel acquired a reputation here among perceptive readers. The issuance of this larger collection of his stories is a literary event of major significance. Now American readers can gain a full sense of his range, his irony, and his torn feelings. As Lionel Trilling observes in the introduction:

There is a contrast in his outlook on and feeling for life. He was captivated by the vision of two ways of life; the way of violence and the way of peace.

Most of the stories are written from personal impressions and reminiscences. The Cossacks in the horse army, Jews in Odessa, Polish Jews in a war-torn land are etched with an almost miraculous economy. A world of change and violence is re-created impressionistically but with an overpowering sense of reality. The pain of change and death. The destruction of war and revolution is seen in contrast to the tale of lives among the Odessa Jews during the period of Babel's boyhood. But even here, there was the violence of the pogroms. In two of the Odessa stories, "The Story of My Dovecot" and "First Love," pogroms are described from the standpoint of the memory of a sensitive boy. These are among the most remarkable of Babel's stories. "The Death of Dolgushov," one of the tales of the horse army, tells of a wounded comrade who wants the coup de grace delivered him. Babel cannot bring himself to fire the shot. A cossack comrade does and then says to Babel: "Get out of my sight, or I'll kill you. You guys in specs have about as much pity for chaps like us as a cat has for a mouse."

In these few swift pages are concentrated the feelings of an imaginative man in an era where change is marked by death, destruction and violence that seem to be part of the natural order of things. Babel is able to give a concentrated revelation of feelings and inner conflicts; and at the same time, to render these on an objective surface which seems overpoweringly real.

Babel's stories are among the great works of literature of our century. The free world should give to this writer the recognition stolen from him by a police state.

1955

Nelson Algren's
A Walk on the Wild Side

Nelson Algren's first short story appeared in *Story Magazine* in 1933. He was a migratory laborer in the Southwest at the time. He won immediate recognition among writers, critics and publishers. Two years later his first novel, *Somebody in Boots,* was published. A powerful work, it remains one of the books of the 1930s which is likely to outlive its own time.

Since then, Nelson Algren has published four other works of fiction. *Never Come Morning, Neon Wilderness* (a collection of short stories), *The Man With The Golden Arm,* and now, *A Walk On The Wild Side.*

Algren has won much recognition. *The Man With The Golden Arm* was described by *Time Magazine* as "one of the finest novels of the year . . . ." Ernest Hemingway predicted that Nelson Algren would rank "among our best American novelists." The praise and recognition is not unmerited; Algren is a writer of definite and genuine talent. The question of recognition is secondary, incidental here. It is of more importance to try and understand what the writer is and to gain some sense of the nature of his books. In his latest novel, Algren gives us help in understanding him. The jacket blurb quotes him: "*A Walk On The Wild Side* wasn't written until long after it had been walked. That was through what remained of old Storyville by the summer of 1931. I'd come to New Orleans with a card entitling me to some editorial position because I'd attended a school of journalism. I wasn't sure whether I wanted to be a columnist or a foreign correspondent but I was willing to take what was open. What was open was a place on a bench in Lafayette Square if you got there early. I found my way to the streets on the other side of the Southern Pacific station where the big jukes were singing something called 'Walking the Wild Side of Life.' I've stayed pretty much on that side of the curb ever since."

Much of Algren's fiction is concerned with those who stay close to the curb. The world he describes is a fringe one of aimless men, prostitutes, junkies, small-time confidence men, petty law-breakers, and the inhabitants of what is usually called Skid Row. For these people Algren possesses a sympathy which can at times flow over into sentimentality. He understands them. His ear for their speech patterns, their ways of thinking, and their frequently twisted outlook on the world, on society, on events and other characters is excellent. Algren not only writes good dialogue but he writes many kinds of good dialogue. The Characters on the West Side Chicago in his *The Man With The Golden Arm* speak in words which ring true and convincing. His Southern procurers, prostitutes, and drunks seem to speak with an equally convincing ring of reality.

A Walk On The Wild Side is mainly concerned with a shambling Southern illiterate, Dore Linkhorn. Uneducated, the son of a preaching father who's "touched," Dore takes to the road. From Texas, he gets to New Orleans and, for a period, he becomes something of a character in the New Orleans *milieu* of prostitutes, panderers and related types of the New Orleans old French Quarter. Dore works as a door-to-door canvasser gyping housewives. He performs as the main actor; a stud horse, as it were, in a peep show operation. He shacks up for a while with a mulatto girl who, although a prostitute, is more than a cut above the other girls in the bordello. He does time after being caught in a raid. He is beaten and blinded in a fight with a legless strong man from whom he had taken the mulatto girl.

In the end, he goes home, back to his origins, seeking the first girl he ever knew.

Algren's novels are atmospheric. More than telling a story, he creates an atmosphere. He writes all around a character and gradually you realize that his character is real and believable. He is atmospheric and impressionistic. Here, his book is slow in getting off the ground. But after he lands Dore in New Orleans, Algren is at his best. He creates characters of the type that most readers have never known. The atmosphere of a brothel is established to the degree that the reader can feel that he knows the place.

Nelson Algren is something of a poet; his talent is poetic. He can lavel poetic feeling on objects, sights, scenes, and areas where few would find anything poetic or lyrical. He can make what is among the most drab of *milieu* change on the printed page. At times, there is a descent into pathos. He can overdo this poeticizing of the drab. Because of this, his writing is uneven and you are alternately moved, lifted up and then dropped down flatly into an unexpected pool of sentimentality.

Concerning *A Walk On The Wild Side,* Algren states: "This is a story that tries to tell something about the natural toughness of women and men, in that order. I like to think it is really about any street of any big town in the country. The book asks why lost people sometimes develop into greater human beings than those who have never been lost in their whole lives."

Algren tells us something about himself here, as a writer, and about the underlying nexus of feelings which dictate his observation and insight. *A Walk On The Wild Side* is not about any street in any big city of the country: it is about any street of the lost in a big city. Here is a combination of both sympathy and sentimentality. Algren is a chronicler of the lost but a chronicler whose talent is definite and unmistakable. He is a gifted but uneven writer. All of his novels seem equally uneven but all of them reveal his special talent and give their reward.

A Walk On The Wild Side is the product of a distinguished American writer.

1956

Edwin O'Connor's
The Last Hurrah

The Last Hurrah is one of the best American novels that I have read in quite some time. Politics has been scarcely touched by American writers of recent decades. Mr. O'Connor has drawn on the drama of American politics for his story. However, it must be stressed that *The Last Hurrah* is primarily a novel. Politics is integrated into the story and the characterizations are sound, plausible; they ring with truth.

The locale for the book is an American city such as Boston. Much of the nature of the city is revealed—the conflicts and differences of generations, and the manner in which changing social attitudes affect American political life and the old-style political machine.

Mr. O'Connor writes of the Irish in politics. He writes with truth and objectivity; at the same time, his characterizations are saturated with warmth. The chief protagonist is the aging mayor Frank Skeffington. Although a fictional creation, Mayor Skeffington suggests a well-known figure in American city politics. He has been mayor for so long that he has come to feel he owns the city. Bold, charming, intelligent, cynical, warmhearted, cruel for political reasons, he is a rogue, but a rogue interestingly and understandingly created.

The story centers around the last campaign of Mayor Skeffington. The Protestant business leaders of the city, the old Cardinal, local politicians, and many of the younger people are against Skeffington. But Skeffington campaigns with boldness and assurance, convinced that he will be victorious. He is of another era, that of machine politics built up on the support of the immigrant and first generation vote.

Skeffington loses, but with a certain grandeur that is integral in his personality. The real architect of his defeat is the late President Roosevelt. The New Deal has cut the ground from under men of Skeffington's political character.

The novel tells the dramatic story of a campaign. It is rich with characters and types. Mr. O'Connor's ear for dialogue is as excellent as his grasp of characters.

This book will be a popular success. It is a pleasure to see a serious and honest young writer receive merited rewards. And this will happen with *The Last Hurrah*, a book studded with keen insight both into politics and human nature, especially Irish human nature.

1956

Writers with Few Readers

The situation and circumstances for writers are incomparably better in America than in most countries. The writers of most other nations, already burdened as they are, have yet in the future to face the full force and to feel the full impact of technological change. In the present, they face problems somewhat different from those which bedevil many of us American writers. These facts can be best seen in the under-developed and in the small countries, where the weight of economic and technological problems seems almost like that of a boulder on a thin roof. In turn, this is affecting patterns of life, the channeling of intellectual and emotional energy, and the very way in which people feel and think. All over the world, there is a serious, and in some cases a desperate, need for trained technical skills. Factories must be built: slums must be cleared. Problems of production, irrigation, the building of dams, the manufacture of military weapons, aeronautics: these fields attract an increasing number of people, and those who go into them receive the highest rewards. And in the solution of problems, the findings of the statistician are coming to be more highly regarded than the impressions of the novelist. All of this, in turn, means that more of the resources of a country flow into these fields and that correspondingly less go into the humanities. This affects writing and culture in many ways.

The writers in small or in under-developed countries suffer because their market is much too limited. Almost all of them must take jobs and do their creative work in their spare time. Thus, I know an Indian novelist who writes in Mahratti, one of the languages of India. He works as a clerk until ten at night, and then writes. I know a young woman in Karachi who became a famous Urdu writer at the age of twenty-one. She earned a thousand rupees on her first book. Today she works for the Pakistani government, and can do little writing. Gavan Casey, one of Australia's leading writers, finds it necessary to devote the greater part of his energies to journalism.

For the writers of many countries, the barriers of language create major obstacles. For instance, how many Dutch and Danish authors can hope to have their work translated into the most-used languages? Unless they are translated, their reputations will remain strictly local. In India, there are fourteen languages, and many of the leading Indian authors write in one of them. Unless these authors are translated into other Indian languages, they can be read only by a very small number of their own countrymen.

The problem of translation is a difficult one because, obviously, there is not the money for publishing a large number of translations in the various languages of India. Further, the opportunity for these writers to be translated into the language of one of the major countries is relatively rare. How many people are there in America, Britain, France who are up to translating books from, say, Urdu, or Mahratti? Whenever possible, the authors try to have their books translated at home and then submitted to foreign publishers. But these translations are usually bad and the authors cannot afford the cost of many translations.

Most small nations and the under-developed countries must be at least bilingual. The language of at least one or more of the major countries is essential for the international life of these countries. Without French or English, and now also Russian, these countries cannot carry on commercial, diplomatic, and cultural relationships. One consequence of this is that writers from the major countries are very well known in most small or under-developed nations. They are often more widely read and discussed than are native writers. The sales of their books interfere with those of local writers. The writers of these countries, correspondingly, are finding their own audience further reduced.

Conditions like these produce psychological confusion. For whom should the authors write? For their own people, or for a foreign market? Despite growing nationalism in Asia, numerous writers and intellectuals have not shed their sense of cultural inferiority towards the West. Just as at one time, American writers needed recognition in England or France in order to become more widely accepted in America, so do many of these writers need foreign recognition. And they hope to escape from other work so that they might give their full time to writing. Because of this their eyes are on the American market. They tend, thus, to become divided in feeling. The pulls of East and West are strongly registered in their minds: some are even torn by this problem, especially because of rising nationalist spirit.

We in America developed a realistic literature at a time when the Republic was so secure that criticism and exposure, even in pitilessly realistic novels, did not weaken the foundations of the nation. It is different in the new countries of Asia. These countries are struggling to become nations. Their leaders and many of their intellectuals are acutely sensitive to the backwardness of their own countries. Last June, in a conversation I had with Mr. Nehru in New Delhi, he remarked that it is humiliating to speak constantly of India's under-development. How critical should Indian writers be? Can they write with the fearless realism and desire for truth of a Zola, or of some of the twentieth century American novelists? If they do, will they not be weakening their own countries?

Writers are conscious of this problem as one of moral dilemma. And the same problem is true in other countries. When I was in Karachi and in Jerusalem, Pakistani and Jewish writers and intellectuals also recognized and admitted the existence of this same moral dilemma.

In a world of rapid change and danger, the human mind lags behind events more than normally. This raises the question of the assimilation and digestion of experience as it relates to creative writing. It is a problem all of us face at all times. But it is perhaps exceptionally difficult in Asia. There, the younger generation of writers has lived through war, independence, the cold war, and the beginnings of an effort at rapid industrialization. Some of them are refugees. Until the writer gains a sense of artistic distance, he usually finds that many of his experiences and impressions are unmanageable for artistic purposes. And much of the present Asian reality remains unmanageable for writers: it has not been fully assimilated and digested.

Finally, these circumstances, problems and dilemmas open cultural pathways for the Soviet Union. Because they are totalitarian, both the Soviet Union and the Chinese Communist governments can easily use money for purposes of cultural influence and infiltration. They can pay for translations: they can give writers magic red-carpet trips to China and Russia. They can provide with facility an international apparatus for the writers of small and new countries. Through their apparatus, they can make the names of writers known abroad, just as they have made Howard Fast a world figure in literature. And they can offer a market of one-third of the world to writers who are frustrated because of a small audience.

The West as a whole, and the United States as the leading Western power, has never been able to set up the effective organizations and the means for cultural dissemination which the Soviet Union can with such ease. This places Russia at an advantage culturally. Further, most of us oppose the use of literature and culture as a means of political propaganda. We see in this, danger or even the death of culture. But with the Russians the political use of culture is both official doctrine and practice. And the fact that the influence of Marxism is strong in so many countries makes the politicized use of culture acceptable to many Asian writers and intellectuals, and even to a considerable number in Europe.

In the last analysis, a writer does and will go on because he *must*. The serious writer continues because he has a driving inner need to try and create. But his problems, both inner and outer, can be more or less difficult according to conditions and circumstances. Today these have definitely become more difficult than they once were. And this has developed at a time when we truly want to literally have a world market, a world audience for literature.

1956

From Bunk to Buncombe

Recently, I reread H.L. Mencken's six volumes of *Prejudices,* which were published during the 1920s, and I am prompted to offer a few observations. In some ways, these present years are like those of the twenties when many of us were young, and it was exciting even to be disillusioned. True, the land is filled with more bunk now than then. But the cult of Inspiration now as then is a profitable enterprise: money in the bank. The ideals of business were the inspiration of national politics in the era of Mencken's *Prejudices* and that has not changed. President Coolidge apparently slept more than President Eisenhower, or than probably any other Chief Executive in the national history, but then, President Eisenhower plays more golf than any of his predecessors. If there is anything to choose between the late Andrew Mellon and Secretary of the Treasury Humphrey, Mellon at least had an art collection; and there was always the chance that Andy Mellon might have had his tongue in his cheek. There was a Hoover in the Cabinet in the days of Coolidge, and now we have temporarily and for some weeks more, a Hoover in the State Department. I cannot quite find a contemporary counterpart to the late Senator Simeon Fess. Congress may boast of many men who are his match in mediocrity, but I am prejudiced in favor of Fess. I have had a fixed idea from my youth that he attained the ultimate in mediocrity. Of course, in the twenties, we did not have any figure remotely comparable to Vice President Nixon. Like flip-top boxes and deodorants, he is wholly new. "Hell and Maria" Dawes seems like an individualist in retrospect—a Bohemian, even an egghead in the present dispensation, although as we saw in those bygone days he was ordinary enough. Of course there was Vice President "Indian Charlie" Curtis. He *would* fit in today, perhaps as a director of culture—organizing a people-to-people campaign to sell America.

Our style today does not seem to me better than it was in the 1920s: it is only different: the Elks Club incoherence of the late Mr. Harding and the meaningless coherence of the advertising fraternity. In the twenties many of the mighty minds were not opposed to books or ideas as much as they were disrelated to such a world. I believe even the Honorable Simeon Fess wrote a book, although no one remembers it. Today, one suspects that the noble Romans of Washington actively dislike books and ideas. By comparison, you almost come to think that the men of past days were touchingly innocent.

The 1920s were gaudy. Preposterousness was close to dramatic. In its place we have sanctimoniousness. It is as though in many areas of life we have gone from the Reverend Billy Sunday to the Reverend Billy Graham. I can imagine some of the statesmen of the 1920s consorting with Billy Sunday and even allowing the grand old foe of Satan to shout some of the devil out of them before they snuck off to take a snort of the fluid they had, by law, made so attractively illegal. But I cannot imagine them asking the advice of Billy Sunday on politics. If they had consulted Billy Sunday it would be to discourse on Sin and the Evil Eye, not on the political situation in the Netherlands or Australia.

In the 1920s, there was less complacency. For instance, the war against the Devil was conducted with a vigor that would probably be ruled out today as too controversial. Problems were simpler, there was no grave international crisis. The Kellogg-Briand Pact was signed outlawing war, but most Americans did not know about it. They did not worry about anti-Americanism; a Hindu was some kind of high-brow whom the wife could have to lecture for the local ladies club. An Arab was as enviable as Rudolph Valentino and someone to keep your wife away from. The French were frogs who didn't pay their debts and had anyone proposed economic aid programs he would have probably been tarred and feathered. The second Senator Lodge was a youth and perhaps a little smarter than he has ever been since.

But these are details. The present is comparable to the twenties in one important sense: it is to the twenties as maturity is to adolescence. The gospel of Service has become more than accepted: it has become intellectually respectable. Platitudes have become the highest wisdom. Dullness has become excitement. The tendencies which Mencken attacked with the best invective ever written in America are winning out. Mediocrity is mass produced: automation is next. Esteemed big men need ghost writers and ghost thinkers even to write the platitudes which had withered on the vine before anyone even knew that the late Honorable Simeon Fess was a mediocrity. And with all this we are developing a higher faculty: the capacity of being bored and loving it.

The twenties were only a forecast. George F. Babbitt has learned how to wear a Brooks Brothers suit. And to laugh you must generally do it alone or in private. There are scarcely any publications which would allow you to do it in public. Mediocrity has elevated itself to the level of sanctification: to challenge it is to commit what is almost the new sin against the Holy Ghost—the sin of controversy. Nero fiddled. Today Mediocrity repeats the hollow platitudes of hope in the voices of a thousand Hollywood reincarnations of Moses on a thousand Sinais and unto each has been given a microphone.

1957

Harvest of O'Faolain

Sean O'Faolain is now fifty-seven. He has been with us for a long time. As a biographer he is not as widely recognized as he deserves to be, and, for instance, you rarely run into persons who have read his unforgettable biography, *Constance Markievicz*. I read it in Dublin almost nineteen years ago but to this day, it remains vivid and alive in my memory. And his work on Daniel O'Connell, *King of the Beggars*, contains some passages which I consider to be among the finest penned by an Irishman in the whole post-Joycean period of Irish literature.

Unlike so many of his contemporaries, he has remained in Ireland and continued to write. This is most difficult and Eire's literary men have been, almost all of them, wild geese. Not only economically, but socially and morally, the lot of the Irish writer who remains at home is a pretty hard one; it is easy for his thoughts and feelings to become distorted by anger and bitterness. This has not happened to O'Faolain. Besides the skill, the insight, the fine style which he brings to his work, you recognize on reading and rereading him that his perspective is balanced. He has an eye for the comic as well as the sad, a good ear for Anglo-Irish speech, and the heart to feel with his characters.

The Finest Stories of Sean O'Faolain consists of thirty tales selected by the author. They range from stories written in his twenties to the most recent ones. He has refused to rewrite some of the earlier pieces—although they are studded with purple patches—because these reveal a part of what he was. A romantic feeling for the countryside and the atmosphere, dawn and twilight, the disillusionment which a sensitive Irishman felt after the Black and Tan war and "the troubles," the simple and often so amusing people of Ireland—these are among the ingredients of his work. Especially, it should be noted, O'Faolain writes of love with extraordinary taste and a grasp of the range of feelings which men and women possess for one another.

Like Yeats, Sean O'Faolain improves with age. He is saturated with a sense of Ireland, but he is not parochial. He is a literary man of the world whose stories reveal the true dignity and the reality of some of his people. In this age of literary deadness and pretense, the re-publication of these stories of Sean O'Faolain takes on the character of a literary event. The word "finest" is not at all misplaced in the title of this book. These are some of the *finest* stories written in English during the last quarter century.

1957

Harvey Swados:
A Veblen of the Novel

Recently, while I was travelling in Europe and Asia, I was often asked to recommend the works of younger American writers. Unfortunately, I have not, in recent years, had the time to read as much new fiction as I would have liked. And some of what I have read has been very tame and disappointing.

The pressure of work caused me to miss the emergence of a most promising new writer, Harvey Swados. His first novel, *Out Went the Candle*, appeared in 1955, but I have just now begun to read it, after reading Swados' second novel, *On the Line*. I found the new book exciting in a quiet way. It is exciting because of its truth, its revelation of a sensibility on the part of the author, its technical and constructive skill, and the simplicity with which Harvey Swados has treated a complicated and difficult subject matter—the life and the feelings of factory workers on an assembly line.

The fuss about proletarian writing in the 1930s is still remembered. The unbelievably bad novels written then are now condemned categorically, but there is scarcely a young person alive who has actually read them. The very phrase, "proletarian novel" is misleading, and it would still be so even if the Communists had not used it as a means of dragooning writers into celebrating the party line. Harvey Swados has written about workers in a factory, and though his work reflects the constructive contribution which the union—obviously the UAW—has made to the life of the worker, *On the Line* should not be categorized or allowed to go unread on this account. This is a skillful literary performance by a young man who writes with the greatest of ease and charm.

Style is not everything in writing, but Harvey Swados is a stylist—to such a degree that some readers may not recognize his true depth. For an easy, graceful and charming style, with flow, movement and variety sometimes confuses people and causes them to think a work may be light and less meaningful than it is.

It is a fascinating and disturbing experience to visit a factory and to watch men working at the line. The pounding noise, the monotony of the work, the seeming confusion where there is order and plan cannot be assimilated on one visit. And if you are a writer and visit a plant, you wonder and ponder as to how you would describe this plant. It is a severely difficult task, but Harvey Swados has mastered it. He has re-created the atmosphere of a factory and a belt or assembly line with such ease that you can even fail to recognize the difficulty of his accomplishment.

Swados takes nine characters, eight working men and one foreman, whose one common bond is the fact that they work on the assembly line in an auto plant. Some of the workers dream. They want to get out of it. They work only because of the wages and because they can use their money to get along in life. Others, older ones, have been caught in the plant and know that they will be there until they are old and can retire with their pensions. One of them works furiously because by so doing he feeds his ego. One is a reformed drunk who has thrown his life away. One is a Negro who wants to sing but whose voice has been irretrievably damaged in an accident. Another is a charming Irish school-teacher who, at first, is fascinated by America and our freedom, but who then decides that he should go back to the poor village in Western Ireland where he taught. Still another is a man who escaped from the line, went into business, failed and must return at the age of fifty-six. Each of the nine emerges as a credible human being, and we sympathize with them all.

The nine men are described in what can be called separate short stories. But each story flows into the next one so that the book has movement, psychological movement as well as the movement which is a result of careful construction and conception. Description, dialogue, exposition are all fused, and you have scene and setting as well as character.

Swados is fair, honest and gifted with insight, also he is a man of taste. This taste is apparent in his refusal to melodramatize and overwrite.

His book is full of small details which reveal how much the union has accomplished positively in easing the lives of the men, men who do hard

work. But his objectivity is unmarred and unbroken, and he conveys a
sense of fate—the fate of those who work at desensitizing and psychologically hurtful work in order that our prosperous society can maintain itself. His picture is disturbing. But what is disturbing is not a peculiarly
American phenomenon: it is a disturbing feature of what we call progress.
The machine has freed man from back-breaking labor. But the machine has
also imposed a discipline of the clock on man which disturbs, distorts and
even embitters his nature. This was one of the major insights of Thorstein
Veblen in *The Instinct of Workmanship.* By artistic re-creation, Swados
has made emotionally comprehensible some of the best of Veblen's insights.

1957

How Should We Rate Dos Passos?

THE GREAT DAYS, **BY JOHN DOS PASSOS**

John Dos Passos is one of the few living American writers who is a world figure. Abroad, his books are sometimes cited as criticisms of American capitalism and as novels which expose American claims and propaganda. At home, Dos Passos is now regarded by some of his former admirers as a man who has made a complete turn, and has abandoned liberalism for the extreme right; he has gone from *The New Republic* to *The National Review.* In consequence, he is regretfully considered as writing in a state of *rigor mortis,* and tears—mostly of the crocodile variety—are shed for him. He is a source of shame and danger to the Madison Avenue psychological warriors who would defeat the Kremlin by selling the USA as though it were the biggest cake of perfumed soap in history; his books are not very useful to the People-to-People geniuses and cannot be sent through the gaping holes of the Iron Curtain with as much success as can stamp kits and hobbycraft chat. And he cannot be cited as a novelist of the liberal spirit, fighting reaction and perpetuating the New Deal spirit. Therefore, he is a good man gone wrong. And a good man gone wrong is, *ipso facto,* unworthy of consideration as a man of letters. Dos Passos' liberalism has so decayed that his lifetime of work is not as important as two short stories and one wooden novel by Lionel Trilling. His credentials as a writer might just as well be taken away from him and he might best be forgotten. He is no longer one of us. He cannot write anyway because the new critics do not study him and Mark Shorer probably would not approve of him.

Thus the level of concern for a writer in this Republic after it has

come of age, lost its innocence, become a world leader. Thus the destiny
of any man who is guilty of the sin of disillusionment. You must be for
something, because in both the liberal and the conservative camps, there is
no political future for one who is not for something. After some decades
of trying, we have failed even in convincing our friends that a novelist does
not necessarily have to be for, and that a writer should not be judged in
terms of immediate political considerations. It is in vain. Philistinism and
self-righteousness are too numerous to be destroyed.

Dos Passos deserves reconsideration and his recent novel, *The Great
Days,* helps us to see what he is about. In his own feeling, he is a libertar-
ian. During his long literary career, he has been concerned with bigness.
Bigness and liberty are not easily compatible. Dos Passos has always been
a novelist of disillusionment, and this is central in his thinking. "War,"
wrote Randolph Bourne, "is the health of the state." Bourne, whose example moved Dos Passos in the 1920s, was writing in criticism of the liberals who supported the American entry into the First World War, and who
believed that the war and the victory over Hohenzollern Germany could be
used to further democratic and liberal ends, thereby making "the world
safe for democracy," or at least more safe. While the Second World War
was already in progress, Dos Passos wrote of "the angry young men" of
the post-war world of the 1920s; he was one of them himself. He said, in
The Ground We Stand On:

... we mustn't forget that they were right to be angry, the American republic was just another piece of stage scenery, so crudely painted as to deceive only the rankest suckers, that masked a slaughterhouse of industrial
exploitation. They [the angry young men of the post-Versailles world]
had seen the physical power of lies to kill and destroy. To men who still
had the smell of blood and rotting flesh in their nostrils any chance seemed
worth taking that might lead to a better world.

Dos Passos' reputation really was established with his novel of post-
war disillusion, *Three Soldiers.* To this day, it remains one of the very best
of twentieth century American war novels, and it describes the ordinary
soldier trapped in the army machine, one of the instruments of the state
grown healthy in war. Here, we find the theme of bigness, bigness in which
the individual is lost, developed as a cause of disillusion. That Dos Passos
was fascinated by bigness is apparent from the experimental novels which
followed *Three Soldiers. Manhattan Transfer* attempted to make the city,

New York, the chief protagonist of a novel, and the trilogy, *USA,* was Dos Passos' attempt to characterize America. In the famous portraits of real figures in *USA,* there is a contrast between the lonely liberals and radicals who thought and fought and lost, and the men of power and money. Bourne and Veblen and Big Bill Haywood in contrast to Woodrow Wilson and Henry Ford. And there is the ultimate victim, Wesley Everett, murdered by a Legion mob, and there is the Unknown Soldier.

Out of the war came a period of the big money and the big power. Some of the angry young men looked to Marx and the Soviet Union, but before a new hope could be assimilated, a new type of bigness had been exposed. Class war and civil war, in Russia and Spain, again reveal the health of the state or its equivalent. Power and lies crush the individual. From *USA* to *One Man's Story* the theme of disillusionment extends. The hope of those lonely and defeated ones, the Veblens, Bournes and Haywoods, is muted; it fades. Out of the *USA* which Dos Passos sought to frame in his trilogy, there came the New Deal, offspring of the New Freedom, and out of that world which disillusioned him in his young manhood, there came the Second World War.

The Great Days is a panoramic novel of the Second World War and its aftermath. However, Dos Passos tells the story and unfolds his panorama through the memory, experience and changing fate of a famous journalist. Ro Lancaster is 59, and in the post-war world, he has become a has-been. Drawing all his money, $3000, from the bank, he flies to Cuba with a redheaded gal who is thirty years his junior, physically striking, lost and frigid. Elsa is like a daughter of a character from *USA.* Lancaster seeks to refind love, but he is too old, too marred by experience. The seeds of disillusion are planted deep. The action of the novel ensues on two planes, present and past. Lancaster, going downhill, remembers the Great Days. These are recalled in terms of his own past, his love for his wife, Grace, who died of cancer, their life together, and the scenes and events he has witnessed as a reporter. This permits Dos Passos to describe wartime Washington, war and the functioning of the supply line in the Pacific, the Nuremburg Trials, post-war Paris. And since Dos Passos is an excellent journalist, his description of the Great Days is vivid. One of his characters, Robert Thurloe, new Secretary of Defense, clearly suggests Forrestal.

But the Great Days are over and Ro Lancaster is one of yesterday's celebrities. He sees, in the rise of Soviet power, newer and graver dangers than those of the past. His trip to Havana is a mistake and, broke, he puts the girl on a bus in Milwaukee; he sinks into the nondescript crowd in the bus station. A full circle has been travelled. From the soldier caught in the gears of the big army machine of World War I, Dos Passos has pursued the themes of liberty and bigness through to the present; his fading celebrity slips back into a life of commonness and anonymity.

John Dos Passos writes with great ease and he is technically inventive. He has conceived various means to write the story of his times as he sees it. *The Great Days* is a well and even an ingeniously constructed book. It is remarkable to think of how much it takes in, because the novel is only of normal length. Dos Passos has always been best at establishing scenes, rather than in portraying characters with depth and strong individuality. The characters reflect a world that is constantly changing, bringing failure and defeat.

Ro Lancaster had written a book, *Blueprints For the Future.* "Nobody read it. What's the use of writing things nobody reads. . . . All that was left of our hopes of those days was a nightmare, a nightmare often recurrent. . . . The whole implacable ocean pours out past that sandspit, sweeping me away, sweeping me to oblivion. . . ." This is Ro. The broken hopes of youth and of the days when this century was young have never been repaired. The expectations of the Wilsonian period have never been recovered. The later disappointments of the New Deal and the Second World War and the post-war era arouse less anger and, in the end, there is resignation. This is the sense of Dos Passos' writing as I can gauge it. He has honestly recorded the play of hope and disappointment over four decades. He has done this with dignity and seriousness.

The future will tell how right or wrong he has been, and I personally think and respond differently than he does. From *Three Soldiers* to *The Great Days,* we can see in Dos Passos the effort of one man of talent and sensibility to take hold of this changing play of forces in our life. It is worthy of new attention and a fresh evaluation. Dos Passos' work is a true, constructive achievement.

1958

The Letters of H. L. Mencken

H.L. Mencken was touched with the quality "greatness." He should go down in the history of our times as one of the few outstanding writers of an era. He could write with an accumulating power that sweeps you along, laughing with him at what you believe in, which happens to be the object of his attack. There was in Mencken the stuff of which a Swift or Voltaire is made. However, the times in which he lived precluded his writing on the level of either a Swift or a Voltaire.

H.L. Mencken came upon the scene when the role of the journalist, the critic, the satirist, the man of letters was being narrowed down. The means as well as the need to do what his true predecessors had done were no longer there. The process of a developing mass-circulation press had already begun. The modern city had already become a phenomenon of society and life was already becoming complex. The pace of change was rapid even though it has since been accelerated.

There was no class or group to look toward a Mencken in order to read its own thoughts expressed with indignation with Mencken's easy erudition, his rich variety of reference and allusion, his humor that revealed an imagination that, if only in an incipient state, was on the level of the artist's.

Mencken needed to find an audience and mold into a coherency strangers who did not know of each other's existence but who had thoughts and feelings growing out of a common ground. Bigness had already become an octopus to claw at the full man and the full mind.

Looking back upon the years of Mencken's life, it seems almost impossible that a man could have become a Voice as Mencken did. The way he did this is a striking indication that he was a man with gifts and ability far and away beyond most men of his generation.

His letters, therefore, take on a great importance. For they give us flashes of Mencken in his various roles. And Mencken had many roles. He was a working journalist, a columnist, a magazine editor, a scholar, a book reviewer and literary critic, an essayist, a humorist and satirist, a translator and an all-around commonsense thinking person with an extraordinary curiosity. There was in him a buoyancy of spirit, an excess of ego, a linguistic flair as well as vigor and discipline.

His letters, accordingly, should have a widespread appeal. They should be read, for many reasons; but the principal reason is that they are good reading. They are simpler in style than his other writing but there is the same pungency and lucidity which were two of his greatest assets. The directness of his language in some of these letters is a refreshing revelation of a certain modesty which was as much a part of his character as were his pride and his vanity.

His letters, accordingly, should be read, for many reasons; but the principal reason is that they are good reading. They are simpler in style than his other writing but there is the same pungency and lucidity which were two of his greatest assets. The directness of his language in some of these letters is a refreshing revelation of a certain modesty which was as much a part of his character as were his pride and his vanity.

Mencken was a prolific letter writer. He is supposed to have written or dictated at least fifty thousand letters. The task of editing a selection of them would be, therefore, taxing. This edition, of course, is not a definitive one. Mencken's papers are sealed until 1975. But Guy J. Forgue, a French scholar from the Sorbonne, has done a fine job of selecting and annotating these. The selection is good; the book has form and continuity.

1961

W. A. Swanberg's *Dreiser*

When Theodore Dreiser died, H.L. Mencken had this to say:

"All of us who write are better off because he lived, worked, and hoped." Theodore Dreiser was a great writer, a literary artist of world stature, and he performed the major service of helping to make possible a twentieth-century American literature. His life is part of the history of America; in fact, of world history.

W.A. Swanberg has written a 528-page book about Dreiser. It is a massive chronological compilation of events—a kind of biographical movie in words. The jacket blurb describes the book as a "comprehensive biography." Comprehensive it is; comprehending it is not.

The life of Theodore Dreiser is important because of what Dreiser did with it, not because of a succession of love affairs, personal squabbles, and lost-and-found friendships. With less writing and more understanding, certain events and their chained sequence would have been of interest.

Dreiser was a brooding, introspective, moody, and wondering man. He was not a happy man. A significant aspect of his unhappiness is what he did with it, what he made of it. This is the main point about the life of Dreiser; the one that should not be forgotten. Dreiser's life had significance because of his writing. *Sister Carrie. Jennie Gerhardt. An American Tragedy. The Genius. The Titans. The Financier. Free and Other Stories. The Bulwark.* All his works.

And yet Mr. Swanberg is almost banal when he offers comments about these writings. He seems to find Dreiser's love letters to the seventeen-year-old "Honey Pot" more interesting.

The 528 pages of carefully researched facts present the picture of a man who is often a boor, sometimes vulgar and erratic, and perennially girl-struck. This is a researched book masking as scholarship but it is the Hollywood pattern twisted around and presuming to be more serious. Mr. Swanberg has presented voluminous facts with a denigrating faithfulness to cliché and an under-developed imagination.

The significance of Dreiser's life is lost in this kind of crude empiricism, off-the-cuff profundity, and platitudinist judgmentalism. The main point about the life of Dreiser is that it does have significance.

What Dreiser created is part of his life. His works have saved him from the nameless dead who are gone into oblivion.

Few writers, even great ones, have the rare fortune that befell Theodore Dreiser. Recognizing the obvious fact that Dreiser and his work are inseparable, we can say that Dreiser became a force. Such a force was Balzac. Leo Tolstoy.

Theodore Dreiser was a great writer, an artist. He is committed to the memory of mankind. Neither his death nor his unimaginative colonizers of literature from Philistine can choke his voice into silence. Theodore Dreiser speaks beyond the grave, and his voice is one of lasting human sympathy.

1965

Harold Frederic's
The Damnation of Theron Ware

The Damnation of Theron Ware [1896] is, to my mind, a very important American novel, one which stands up. The characterization of Theron Ware is an acute characterization: I think he is truly a character in American literature. His process of development is dialectical in character. What seems to be growth has within itself the seeds of disintegration. This is further influenced by the fact that Theron Ware takes the advice of Sister Soulsby, and plans to achieve his new life by a compromise, that of keeping within the folds of the faith on the one hand, and of living a rich personal and intellectual and emotional life on the other. Compromise is fatal to him, for the reason that his position as a minister doesn't permit that. It can only cause hypocrisy of a kind that eats into the roots of the soul. We see, but of such factors, how he becomes, instead of one who develops, a person whose development has tended to turn into fatuousness.

It is typical of many clerics that, in their first stages of discovering the possibilities of the world, they go forth to grasp these with a background of adolescent and naive emotions. Theron Ware is emotionally backward, and Harold Frederic is acute and incisive in the way that he concretely documents this aspect of Ware's personality. In a restrained way, the process of self-development of Ware tends to predict the so-called revolt of the twenties, with youth in seeking freedom, going to the extreme of seeking freedom, this being pure personal expression, which in turn becomes quite frequently mere gratification of impulse. The pattern is part of that which often characterizes young manhood and the last so-called stage of adolescence. Ware, on a restrained level, inasmuch as he is a minister, etc., follows through that pattern. Often, Frederic shows real subtlety in his grasp of such phases of Ware's character, and of his "development." Also, the conduct of the heroine, Celia, is extremely interesting to me. In essence, she acts like a rich girl, one who is whimsical, impulsive, concerned with gratifications and possessed of the means of achieving these. Often, such people—because of their wealth, and especially if they are young and feminine—because they are beautiful as well as rich—develop without even thinking of it, an attitude which leads them to tamper irresponsible with other people's lives. In essence, that is what this girl does with Theron Ware. He is basically sincere, and because of his sincerity and his inexperience, he takes things at face value. He doesn't understand the innuendoes, the qualifications, the conventions of expression and attitude of richer and more cultivated people, and he takes these at face and literal value. He acts on them. Herein, we see (a) an important cause of his disintegration, and (b) the role which Celia plays in messing up his life.

Frederic is often called a Populist writer. I wonder why. He is really sophisticated and grasped towards the gain of a sense of world culture. This, itself, makes the book remarkable for its time, if we consider the character of American life when the Gilded Age was coming to its end and creating the material and social basis for the uprise of such human phenomena as that of, say, George Babbitt.

Frederic illustrates the terrible backwardness of American life in this book. So much that is casually accepted by ordinarily experienced and sophisticated people of the city, so much is new, fresh, bewildering to Theron Ware. Just as he is personally immature, so is his whole background socially immature. While the book contains such an excellent characterization, that characterization is, in itself, a fine social characterization also.

The portrait of Dr. Ledsmar is very good. Ledsmar is close to Darwinism, the period of rampant Spencerian influence, the time when scientific discoveries were turned into generalizations about all of life and society, producing fatally incorrect conceptions of characters and events in society. That period, and the times preceding it, produced a rich variety of assumedly scientifically warranted generalizations which were narrow, and often cockeyed. We see something of this in Ledsmar. His attitude towards women, which he bases more or less on biology, is an instance. Ware's attitude towards Ledsmar is very revealing. There we see how out of ignorance, a simple idealistic way of looking at the world, and emotional immaturity, he takes Ledsmar at face value.

Much of what I say of Ware here further comes out clearly as the occupational effect on character. His very profession, Methodist minister, conditions this. Further, again and again, Frederic brings out the occupational effect on character of the sacred profession: Ware's tendency to meet situations of grief, nervous strain, etc., with a bromide; his ease in finding banalities to meet so many occasions; his reaction to the lawyer Gorringe; the kind of false confidence which he carries as a result of the dignity socially attached to his profession; his inclination to oratory, which is a kind of parallel on another level to his literal mindedness. He deals in words. They are his tools. He is a minister of a Christian religion which is literal in its acceptance of words, words in the Bible and the Discipline. This literalness utterly prevents him from grasping any subtleties of character and mind, brought out in human relationships. He understands his wife as badly as he does Celia, the Irish girl. For several centuries, education was purely verbal, a matter of words, and with this verbal type of education there was added authority—particularly and precisely the authority of the Holy Book itself. We see, in Ware's literalness, something of the concrete social meaning, the social cost, the concrete products of this type of education. So much, along these lines, is implied and stands behind the book.

In a very primitive and tentative way, we see in this book and in the times the first stages of change in religious life, mores, etc., that is—at a later time—documented by a type like Elmer Gantry. The influence of money, the pull of the town on the country, the growing hegemony of town over country, all these tendencies are reflected in the novel. There is more religious sincerity in this period, however; thus, Sister Soulsby is different from Reverend Monday.

There is a moral struggle in Theron Ware. By the time that Puritanism is pretty much overwhelmed in the post-war period, this moral struggle passes out. Just as everything that Babbitt buys is standardized. Moral problems don't hit often with acute thrusts. They are cushioned in standardization, in moral precepts and moral homilies. Moral solutions to problems are more or less commodities.

When protest again flares up in writing, it is protest against social conditions, against a general atmosphere which produces a life of spiritual poverty, protest which is, in one way or another, against society and against the cost of American development as that cost is reflected in its effect on individual destinies.

With this development, one theme in writing in America tends to drop out: the theme of self-discovery and self-development.

On the whole, American literature of the last fifty to sixty years had to be re-examined and rediscovered, studied with more perspective and more effort to relate it to the development of American society. If this is done seriously, *The Damnation of Theron Ware* will deserve a long, serious, and detailed analysis.

1967

IV
ON THE CRAFT OF WRITING

On Being an American Writer

Some years ago, I participated in a symposium on the American novel conducted by the Harvard Law School Forum. A writer who had recently written a best seller voiced some complaints about the conditions of writing in America. He claimed that there was something in the atmosphere in America which caused writers to begin with a bright flush of promise; and then, in middle age, to deteriorate and disintegrate. He spoke of writers destroying themselves, even committing suicide. He lamented on the "benefactions" of success. After he had written his best seller, he received invitations to dine with people whom he had not previously known, people who would not have wanted him in their homes if he were not a successful novelist. His time was no longer completely his own. He was much put upon.

I took issue with him. I granted that there were overwhelming dangers of commercialism in American literature. But I pointed out that we had developed a tradition of honesty and integrity in American literature. I cited the American novel as an example. During the present century, there have been many American novelists who have written their best, scorning the commercial formula. They have not only sustained themselves but have also found an audience to help them sustain themselves. I listed Theodore Dreiser, Sherwood Anderson, Sinclair Lewis, John Dos Passos, Ernest Hemingway, Thomas Wolfe, William Faulkner, Erskine Caldwell, and many others. One can like or dislike these writers on grounds of personal taste, literary judgment and content. Withal, it remains that they wrote many books which gave form and expression to what they saw, felt, and believed. The twentieth century American novel has been an example of integrity in a period when we have witnessed the most tremendous development of commercialism of culture in the entire history of mankind. And in addition to these writers whose names have become outstanding, there are hundreds of others in America who seriously, honestly, and sometimes sacrificially, have tried to write books which would tell the truth. This is a frequently overlooked fact about American culture. And it should be one of the prides of those who are seriously interested in seeing the growth of culture in this country.

Recognizing this, I want to talk about the uninspiring aspect of our contemporary culture as it affects a writer. I want to talk to the public and in a loud voice.

I have been a writer for many years. When I began my career, I knew that one of the basic problems which I, as well as other writers, must face is that of truth versus money. I pointed this out in my early articles. Time and time again I wrote that the serious writer must make a choice and take certain risks for truth. I wrote that he must either try to tell the truth and write honestly out of himself, or else he must write for money.

Literature is one of the most powerful means whereby men can talk to men. Basically it is a means of transmitting experience, feeling, and emotion so that one man can tell others, either in the present or in the future, something of the story of how men and women have lived and felt and thought. Through literature, not only the artist but also the reader is able to intensify his awareness and to deepen and expand his understanding. The need for literature is something which can be assumed as axiomatic. For centuries, artists have created a literature for mankind. Dead writers have contributed toward the development of the literature which exists in the world today. The value of literature has been born of the blood, sweat, toil and heartache of countless writers of many lands and many centuries. Literature is the property of mankind.

The writer often occupies an honorable place in the memory of mankind. This is especially true of the dead writer. He is a more convenient person than a living writer. It is easier to honor him and place a halo upon his head.

The history of literature is replete with instances of writers who have been attacked, vilified, neglected, scorned, who have lived in poverty during their lifetime, only to become among the most honored of the honorable dead, once they are no more. Recall the attacks on Shelley. Remember Jefferies. In America, forget not the experiences of Poe, Melville, and Whitman, three of our greatest writers. Pedantic and philistine critics, politicians and clergymen, policemen, a whole human array has from time to time been marshalled against real and original writers. At one time or another, some writers and serious thinkers have merited the attention of the police. Under Hitler and behind Stalin's Iron Curtain, writers (like everyone else) got unremitting attention of the police. Almost every generation of serious writers meets the same types of obstacles. The struggle which each generation of writers must make is repeated again and again. Baudelaire, today honored in France, was once suppressed. Dreiser met constant bitter opposition.

The life of a writer is usually one of permanent insecurity. On the one hand he is in danger of becoming the victim of censors. He does not know at what moment, in what place, a book of his will be threatened with suppression. Sometimes he does not know but when his entire lifework will be threatened with banning.

Another feature of the permanent insecurity of the writer is economic. He is constantly under pressure that could make a literary whore of him.

There is a need for writing but there is no special need for any particular writer. The need must be created for each writer's work. Each writer must, through his books, with what help and attention he gets from critics, reviewers, librarians, book sellers, and others involved in the apparatus of culture, find and contribute toward creating his own audience. This becomes more difficult every year. The market is now being wrecked by junk with publishers competing in the sale of junk. Movies and television encourage junkmen instead of writers.

The story is familiar but many who know it remain cowardly silent. Some are contemptuous of the honest artist because once upon a time, they wanted to be honest men. The writer is alone. He has one alternative. To fight and to win. And the courageous artist cannot lose. He may suffer. He may die miserably as Poe did. But his work has the "strange" power to live.

There is only one kind of writer, he who will fight. The artist who does less betrays himself. Happiness, comfort, even love cannot always be his. But he can attain victory.

1956

Journalism or Creative Writing Course?

Students who want to write ask me if it is wise for them to enter journalism as a means for preparing for a literary career. This is not a question that can be answered with a generalization. The answer depends upon the individual; it will vary from person to person.

In my own beginning years, I had six months' experience as a part-time journalist. I was a campus reporter at the University of Chicago. I don't think that this hurt me; but I have used little of that experience in my fiction. Since then, I have taken shots at various kinds of journalism. I've covered a prize fight, a labor union convention. And I have done some political reporting, and have done some baseball writing. But for the main, I stayed away from journalism except on rare occasions.
baseball writing. But for the main, I stayed away from journalism except on rare occasions.

Now, I find myself reversing the pattern. In the last few years, I have given more time to it.

This suggests a few observations. These may have only a personal reference but for what they may be worth, I offer them:

First, and I have no desire to sound vain or to denigrate reporters, it is easier to be a journalist than it is to produce serious fiction, serious literary criticism, or serious articles dealing with ideas and theories. Journalism may put more strain on your nerves, especially if you are covering dramatic events and must meet a deadline. But this is a passing tension. Writing which deals with ideas puts a heavier, and sometimes a more dangerous, strain on a person. It is a mental, a strong emotional strain. Too, in journalism, your satisfaction comes more quickly. You don't have to live in time, day after day with your subject, delaying your gratifications, sometimes for years. And in journalism you are not as deeply involved as you are in creative writing. While reporting, you are usually outside the event. You are a spectator and in order to write objectively you try to retain your spectatorial relationship. But when you write a serious novel, you are not outside. You are profoundly involved with your characters and their fate. You live in two worlds, the imagined world that you seek to create and the ordinary world around you. You dig into and you touch tender spots of your character, thereby producing anxieties and occasionally stirring dangerous impulses which can crowd into your unconscious mind. There is a moral hazard which is not usually encountered in journalism.

In literary criticism and intellectual analysis, the strain is mental. To think with precision and to express your thoughts is very difficult. The problem of clarity is a major one. That of language is burdensome. In fact, one of the great difficulties in literary criticism is that of language, for the language of literary criticism is already too cluttered with clichés and portemanteau words. So many people discuss literature with received sentiments. The area of indefiniteness is wide; everything you treat can be a subject of varying interpretations. Complexities of thought become intractable when you try to put them down on paper.

For me, literary criticism and fiction writing are more satisfying than journalism. In both cases, you are the master of your own world. And if you don't attain that mastery, it is because of your own limitations. Your ego grows and expands when you believe that you have been relatively successful.

In journalism, your ego suffers constant wounds. Often the journalist must give time and attention to people inferior to himself. He must suffer their vanities and their pomposities. Sometimes the journalist must strain to extract a story from a dunderhead. The journalist's subjects are assigned to him without regard for his own inner impulses. And his work is bounded by numerous restrictions. He is limited in space; he writes under a time schedule. His audience is so vast and so mixed that he must be clear to people on numerous levels of understanding. These factors impose limitations on the free play of mind and restrict an indulgence in wit, satire, and irony. This can be very repressive.

Journalism can be more dangerous. It requires a quickness of mind and an immediate perceptivity. It demands that you assimilate rapidly, even though superficially. It calls for skill and ability and has its own rewards.

But again, and I remind you that I am speaking personally, I do not think that my experience as a journalist has hurt or helped me as a writer. It is just one more experience among many experiences.

1963

The Development of the American Novel

When one considers the fact that countless thousands of American novels have been written since the founding of our Republic, it seems presumptuous to essay the effort to write an essay on the American novel. Besides, I am a practicing novelist and I have other interests which require time for reading. I cannot write on the American novel as a scholar. I could go to the works of scholars and literary historians and repeat what they have written but this would result in my dishing out impressions and information second hand. It would be dishonest; I would be giving as my own judgments the views of others.

Therefore, I shall state some views of my own based on my readings and reflections. Perhaps this will serve as a contribution, a stimulus, towards fresher and fuller study.

Literary opinion and judgment tend to become steroetyped. Successive novelists become the victims of clichés. They are pigeon-holed, rubber-stamped, and packaged off in one or another classification and this serves as a substitute for an individual impression. In my own time as a practicing American novelist, I have witnessed the invention of a number of such clichés. Various novelists have been classified as writers of the twenties, the thirties, or the forties. Certain generalized notions about the character of life and literature during these decades have been accepted as full characterizations of the attitudes and temper of these years; and then, novelists have been interpreted in terms of these generalizations.

For example, I have been rubber-stamped as a novelist of the thirties.

In some instances, I have been treated as though I were born a writer, full-blown, after the stock market crash of 1929. It is as though I had no infancy, childhood or youth which affected and influenced the formation of my consciousness as a writer. It would seem that all I had reacted to was the Great Depression; that it was the major event in my literary career.

Other writers have suffered in the same fashion. They have been locked up in an arbitrarily segmented fraction of time and have been, as it were, decimalized. For literary commentators, critics, book reviewers and editors, there is some kind of magic in each decade. Continuity is journalistically ruptured every ten years; continuity of influence is sacrificed for plausible clichés about the twenties, the thirties, and the forties.

There are other stereotypes besides chronological ones. The words "naturalism" and "realism" have become such. There is talk of the "field of realism" in American literature. There is presumed to be some method that is realistic and naturalistic; and marked by a philosophical attitude of determinism. This places a number of writers in a category. They are naturalists. They constitute a school. This school has exhausted itself. Ergo: these writers have outlived themselves and lack the grace and the decency to permit themselves to be embalmed.

Then there are the sociological clichés. Certain writers are "sociologists," not artists. They practice sociological realism, social realism, and they cure the social evil of juvenile delinquency at a time when juvenile delinquency is becoming a more serious social problem.

Or, they celebrate the "New Deal." A critic speaks of "the liberal imagination." This cliché may be used negatively and a critic may claim that "the liberal imagination" has produced no novels. Or, an editor discovers that no novelist has written about what is called "Joe McCarthyism" or . . . *ad infinitum.*

Now we have a new set of stereotypes being invented more or less as a means of reviving what used to be called the "genteel tradition." We have a new criterion which would treat all writers as though they were John Donne. Books are not what they seem; they are something else. They are symbols and sometimes symbols can be understood; at other times they are too profound for human understanding. Thus a critic reviewing William Faulkner in a literary journal declared that the novel was symbolic of something deep in man, something too deep to be understood.

A novel is a myth; a symbol. It is an allegory; a parable. Some critics are becoming dissatisfied with these clichés and are trying to invent new ones.

The understanding and the reading of novels in America is crippled by these types of categorization. Categories become stereotypes. These become criteria for judging. It is generally accepted that the American novel came of age in the twentieth century. It was generally accepted until the last ten or so years that the main tendency or emphasis in the American novel was that which was called realistic and which was illustrated in such a pioneering writer as Theodore Dreiser. In the last sixty to seventy years, a respectable body of fiction has been produced in this country. There have been Henry James, Harold Frederic, Stephen Crane, Frank Norris, Theodore Dreiser, Upton Sinclair, Jack London, Mary Austin, Sherwood Anderson, Sinclair Lewis, Zona Cale, O.E. Rolvaag, Abraham Cahan, Ring Lardner, Ernest Hemingway, F. Scott Fitzgerald, William Faulkner, John Dos Passos, Thomas Wolfe, Willa Cather, James Branch Cabell, Jo seph Hergesheimer, Glenway Wescott, Erskine Caldwell, Richard Wright, Claude McKay, Nelson Algren, Carson McCullers, and many others. One can like or dislike the writings of any or all of them but I think that it is fair to state that they have written honest and serious novels.

Their names belong in the category of literature. In their respective ways, they have re-created some sense of experience in America. They have created characters out of the fabric of American life.

One can take the works of these, and other writers, and find similarities or differences among them. One can turn them into fragments of a puzzle and piece these fragments into a picture. One can declare that they are to be divided up into realists and romanticists, into social realists and non-social realists, into moral and immoral writers and so on. But I do not think that one worked-out explanation and exposition will exhaust the meaning and significance of their work. In other words, there is not one explanation which can suffice to explain or interpret the American novel. The novels are too varied. There are too many differences in style, attitude, subject matters, locale, and meanings. For every similarity to be found, there are corresponding differences.

1965

The Writer—Neurotic or Psychotic?

Many believe that the writer is neurotic; some believe the writer is even mad. And I am what is called a writer. I have never fully subscribed to any such notions of the writer even though you can, with selective emphasis, make out quite a case to prove that they are—either mad or neurotic.

On the whole, you find a considerable degree of drinking among writers. And some writers have seemed aberrant in other ways. Dostoyevsky was a compulsive gambler. He was an epileptic, too, and according to an assumption of Freud, his epilepsy was psychogenetic. Tolstoy was extremely volatile and short-tempered.

But there are some simple observations to be made concerning writers and their aberrations. More is known of their lives. Writers tell more themselves and biographers dig out much that they might not have told. Too, writers write of emotions which come from deeply embedded inner drives. They often rouse the kind of emotions in themselves which can be dangerous if they are touched off—in anyone. Writers cannot build the same heavy armors against their inner drives that others do because it is precisely these drives which push them to write, and which they must handle in their work.

The serious writer takes on himself when he attempts a major work. And, he takes upon himself the risks from unloosing the gates of all that distresses and troubles him. He is opening some of the doors which close out his unconscious. He is pulling down barriers which wall in his human nature. We are all more or less aware of the fact that in human nature there are constructive and destructive tendencies.

When writers succeed, they often gain greater control over themselves and their work can have a constructive, even therapeutic, effect on them. But they are playing with the fire that is in them. Why? To ask is like asking why a person falls in love. Writers do this because they feel a need to; they feel they must. The need for expression is compelling in them. In my opinion, not a great deal is known about the process of writing. But I believe that what I have written here is true and relevant.

1967

Literature and Dogmatism

What is the function, the role performed by literature? It has been a source of regret to me that I have not had the time to pursue this problem more diligently and to write more than I have on it. But this is the kind of regret we are likely to feel about every one of our interests. We gain only partial knowledge and our conclusions and theories can only be tentative in character. To be dogmatic or absolutistic is to freeze off your mind and to deceive yourself with a conviction of certainty where certainties are quite meaningless. This is especially the case concerning literature. Despite the vast amount which has been written about the subject, it remains mysterious to us. We know little about the so-called creative process. It remains a significant aspect of the greatest of all mysteries, the mystery of man, the mystery of ourselves.

Thinking about literature, both on the journalistic as well as on the academic and theoretical level, is usually partial and dogmatic. Critics and analysts constantly forget or fail to realize that it is risky to speak with finality about literature at any one point of time. Some of them do not draw simple lessons from their own experience. Here and there today we find a new critic dogmatizing with the air of authority, and yet back in the thirties, he was equally certain about the Marxism he now rejects.

Once we have gained a measure of experience in reading, it is usually easy for us to recognize greatness or at least validity and seriousness in works of literature. We can do this even though we cannot offer a clear explanation of why a certain work is great, or at least why it belongs in what

Professor Sculley Bradley has designated as "the category of literature."
Frequently our explanations of why we admire books are strongly deform-
ed by rationalizations. Usually we like and respond before we know why
and can give reasons. No matter how much we formally oppose an impressionistic approach to literature, our actual responses to particular literary
works are definitely marked by impressionism.

There is a simple reason why we have such little certainty in our efforts to explain literature formally and generally. Literature is, or it can
be, as broad as life. It is not confined within boundaries and provinces. It
is a concentrated and powerful means of expression; or as Tolstoy recognized, expressing something of what has been, or is being thought and felt
by men. From generation to generation, it is differently read and interpreted. Over a course of the years, the interpretations of any great and significant writer will be so varied and so contradictory, one with the other,
that neither sense nor order can be made of these interpretations. The fact
that a work of literature can evoke or stimulate such a variety of responses
and interpretations is indicative of the extent and the appeal of literature.
It suggests that literature is all-encompassing and that it cannot be pressed
within the limits of any theory except one which would have such gen-
erality that it can offer support to those who dogmatize. Obviously the
task of explaining literature, or rendering it intellectually comprehensible,
is one of importance. The task of criticism is likewise, important and often valuable.

We continue living in time and even that which is most familiar is
full of surprises. We must perform our intellectual operation on literature
with flexibility, a recognition of the pluralistic character of literature and
a readiness to remain with uncertainties rather than to adopt, and possibly
defend, militantly, a view of such narrow, pseudo-certainties, which the
next generation will toss into the waste basket.

1968

On Ignorance

Some dozen or so years ago, I submitted to a publisher in New York the translation of a book by an Urdu writer. The publisher returned the book to me saying that he knew nothing about Hindus and Muslims. I wrote him and told him, in effect, that he had no right to reject a book on the basis of his own ignorance. It was his duty to find out as much as he could of what he would need to know, and then to get the assistance of others who knew what he did not know.

He did not answer my letter.

Business is business. Business men are busy.

When my first work appeared, a number of the critics did not know what the books were about. They did not like them because of what they themselves did not know. Others distorted my books and interpreted them into meaning what they, the reviewers, had at least a passing familiarity with. This is how Studs Lonigan who lived in a hundred-thousand-dollar apartment house that his father, a self-made painting contractor, owned, became a mid-western fascimile of the lower East Side of New York. This is how the book was labelled a book about slums. And from this, the notion that I was ignorant and uneducated—a lucky natural born, one-shot writer, was accepted.

Thirty years later, evidence of this notion still exists. When my novel *The Silence of History* was published in 1963, it contained many references to Napoleon I. A professor at Northwestern University in Evanston, Illinois, criticized me for my references to Napoleon about whom I was presumably ignorant. I wrote him and said that the American historian Charles A. Beard had praised writings of mine on Napolean and that I had been invited to speak to a cadet class at the Air Force Academy in Colorado on the military history of Napoleon. The professor from Northwestern wrote publicly that since Charles A. Beard had liked my writings on Napoleon, his criticism was erased. (He found other things wrong with me instead.)

Still, I am called bitter when I say that many of the professors, critics, and reviewers are fakers and frauds. When ignorant and lazy men make careers out of the minds and talents of others, what are they? What would you call them?

1970